MIDDLE PARK

THE WAY WE WERE

The Middle Park History Group

Middle Park Historical Series Number Three

ISBN: 978-0-9872241-2-5
Published by Middle Park History Group Inc. © 2016
Editor: Jackie Tidey
Picture Research: Sonya Cameron
Cover design: Lara Cameron
Cover photo: Middle Park Baths
Text design and layout: Vanessa Battersby
Printing: Mercedes Waratah

National Library of Australia
Cataloguing-in-Publication entry

    Middle Park : the way we were / Middle Park History Group.
    9780987224125 (paperback)
    Middle Park historical series ; no. 3.
    Includes bibliographical references.
    Middle Park (Vic.) – History – Anecdotes.

    Other Creators/Contributors: Middle Park History Group

    994.51

The Middle Park Historical Series is one of many projects published in hard
copy or on the web. The Middle Park History Group acts to promote awareness
and preservation of the unique heritage of Middle Park.

To join the History Group or obtain a copy of:
* *The Heart of Middle Park: Stories from a Suburb by the Sea*
* *Middle Park: from Swamp to Suburb*
* *Middle Park: The Way We Were*

please contact:
    The Secretary
    Middle Park History Group Inc.
    PO Box 5276
    Middle Park
    VIC 3206

    Email: middleparkhistorygroup@gmail.com
    Website: http://www.middleparkhistory.org

CONTENTS

ACKNOWLEDGEMENTS

This book, the third by the Middle Park History Group, once again owes its existence to a group of dedicated researchers and local residents – Sonya Cameron, Diana Phoenix, Max Nankervis, Edward Boyle, David South, Anne Miller, Rosemary Goad and Meyer Eidelson. Their chapters were then taken and worked into a whole by our volunteer editor, Jackie Tidey. Lara Cameron was generous with her time in designing the book cover and Vanessa Battersby was employed to design the book layout, ready for publication.

Anne Scambary from the City of Port Phillip was extremely helpful in obtaining high quality digital copies of images from the CoPP Heritage Database. And financial support from the City of Port Phillip has helped with the purchase of images and the costs associated with producing this book.

Individual chapters owe special thanks to specific organisations and people:

- Shops and shopping in Middle Park and the list of former shops – this chapter and the list of shops had its beginnings in a map of some of the shops created by Rosemary Goad and a spreadsheet created by Max Nankervis in which he listed all the occupiers of houses and the types of shops/businesses in the study area (Middle Park and those parts of Albert Park up to Kerferd Road). When the Sands & McDougall directories ended in 1974, Diana Phoenix helped the author by searching categories of shops in the Melbourne Yellow Pages. Sarah Slade, from the State Library of Victoria, has been most helpful and responsive in the request for high resolution images from the 1970s Committee for Urban Action photographic survey of the former South Melbourne.

- Middle Park and The Great War - Maree Wilson and Perce Makin have been sources of information on Les and Jim Makin, in particular providing access to the brothers' wartime correspondence. Joanne Scanlan and Kath Scanlan have generously provided family photos of Les and Jim Makin. Lambis Englezos has explained his research on the 'missing' soldiers of Fromelles.

- Dairies, Manufacturing and Other Light Industries – special thanks to descendants of the various dairymen of Middle Park - Frank Dobeli, descendant of Martin Dobeli's dairy in Herbert Street; Shane Mulligan, grandson of Richard and Mary Mulligan from Bracklyn Dairy at 337 Danks Street; Pat Berger, descendant of Joseph Farnsworth's dairy in Carter Street; and Cam and Laura Hines who have purchased the former Feign Dairy at 45 Patterson Street; and Paul Connor who now lives in part of the former Milkap Factory and who provided details of the building's former life.

- The Greek Immigrants of Middle Park – many Greek immigrants who are now residing in Middle Park have told their stories to the Middle Park History Group. Unfortunately we only have room for three oral histories in this book – from Calliopi Fonias, Aris Yiannakis and Vicky Galinas. Thank you to them and their families for allowing their stories to be told and recorded.

- The Middle Park Bowling Club chapter was researched by author David South with the full cooperation of the Club. He particularly acknowledges the assistance of Bill Sorraghan OAM, RVBA historian. A number of Middle Park Club members also helped a good deal, particularly Peter Anderson.

INTRODUCTION

Most of us who live in Middle Park realise how lucky we are to live in this suburb bounded by sea and park, with its wide, shady streets, varied and distinctive architecture, community-minded residents and ample amenities. It's also our good fortune that living among us there's a dedicated band of amateur and professional historians and writers, the Middle Park History Group, who devote countless hours to researching, investigating and writing books about this place where we live.

The first book – *The Heart of Middle Park* – was designed to take readers on 'a voyage of discovery of iconic places, people and milestones in the life of an Edwardian suburb by the sea.' Appropriately, it was sub-titled: *Stories from a suburb by the sea.* It was well-received and a second project was soon underway. The second book, *Middle Park: From Swamp to Suburb* – was a more ambitious production, 210 pages of text and illustrations, double the size of the first book. It explains how a low, swampy area developed into a pleasant and comfortable suburb with its attractive mix of Victorian, Edwardian and modern architecture.

Now, five years after the first publication, the Middle Park History Group's trilogy of local history is accomplished. Book Three – *Middle Park: The Way We Were* – introduces the reader to daily life as it used to be in our suburb: our early shops and the way we shopped in them, decades and even a century, ago; the role that the beach and bowling club played in our social development; the way the suburb was laid out and developed from the beginning; the disappearances of the milkman and his horse and cart, and a bit later, all the large and small industries that once dotted our suburb. It tells too the stories of some of the young men who went to the Great War and didn't come back, and invites some of our Greek neighbours to tell their own stories of how they left their homeland and came here as migrants in the 1960s and 70s. Lastly, we hear some tales of the darker side of Middle Park, of robbery, mystery and murder.

Readers investigating *The Way We Were* will find much to surprise (and delight) them. Who was Madame Brussels? Where could you swim and sunbathe naked?

Were there really three butcher's shops in Armstrong Street – all at the same time?

What did the Milkap Factory make? Was your house once a shop? Or was your apartment once part of a factory? There is a real sense in these pages of knowing and enjoying what was here before us.

A common purpose links all three publications of the intriguing history of Middle Park: to know the past and share our common heritage so that we can understand the present and help build a better future.

SHOPS AND SHOPPING IN MIDDLE PARK: CHANGES OVER 100 YEARS

Sonya Cameron

In the days before people owned fridges and cars, at the beginning of the 20th century, shopping was a frequent, local and predominantly female activity. The housewife of Middle Park did not have to leave her suburb in order to provide for the daily needs of her family. She could buy food for the family at the local butcher, fishmonger, grocer, greengrocer and fruiterer, bakery, confectioner and dairy. She could clothe her family at the local draper's, visit the local bank, buy new shoes or have the old ones repaired at the bootmaker's, arrange for fuel to be delivered from the wood yard, get her medications and cosmetics from the chemist, borrow a book from one of the private libraries or find a dressmaker, music teacher, dentist, plumber, carpenter, optician or upholsterer – and all within walking distance of her home. Only the wealthy had carriages so she mostly carried her shopping home with her in her wicker basket or string bag – though some shops took orders and arranged delivery. Food was almost entirely unprocessed and unpackaged: meat was chopped from the carcass, butter and cheese were sliced from the block and wrapped in greaseproof paper, biscuits were bought by weight from a large tin, boiled sweets were bought individually from large glass jars. Perishable items such as milk, bread and ice were delivered daily, though the housewife could visit the local dairy with her billycan and buy milk directly. Street vendors also visited, for example the 'rabbito' and the fish-seller. On Sundays a chap from one of the dairies would come by with cream and you could fill your jug at the gate and pay on the spot. Before domestic refrigeration became affordable, the Middle Park housewife would have shopped on a daily basis and stored her perishable items in an ice-chest. Ice-chests or ice-boxes were typically made of wood, lined with tin or zinc and insulated with sawdust, seaweed, wool or cork, and later, asbestos. The ice-man delivered a big block of ice and he usually carried it under his arm wrapped in an old hessian bag. He would place the block in a tray at the top of the unit and as the ice began to melt during the week a pipe for the melted water ran from the ice-tray to a drip-tray underneath the ice-box. The drip-tray had to be emptied daily if you didn't want a pool of water to form on the floor around the ice-box. Food, including meat, milk and butter, could be successfully stored for two to three days. Ice-blocks often lasted a week, not so long in very hot weather.

Middle Park's main shopping area

Middle Park's main shopping and entertainment precinct was centred on Armstrong Street between Canterbury Road and Richardson Street. Middle Park's only hotel stood, and still stands, on the corner of Canterbury and Armstrong Streets and the Middle Park Theatre was next door to the hotel. Today the theatre is being used as a gym studio. There was very little vehicular traffic then and local housewives could stroll leisurely from shop to shop. Substantial verandas of considerable height extended across the entire width of the pavements, not only providing shelter from sun and rain for the shopper but also protecting the goods on display in the windows from fading in the sun. Once cars came into common use, however, there was pressure to remove these verandas as they hindered parking and cars ran into the veranda posts. Their removal meant larger plate glass windows could be installed. (Most of these verandas were removed in Armstrong Street in the early 1970s and have now been replaced by various styles of cantilevered awnings.)

Armstrong Street c. 1920

The Armstrong Street shopping strip, also known as the 'Middle Park Shopping Centre', is described as a 'hive of activity' in the 1940s by Mary Barry in her oral interview. At the time she is speaking about there were three butchers' shops, three chemists (including a large one on the corner of Canterbury Road), three hairdressers (including Alf Weeks's shop where the idea of The Old Buffers' parade began), three fruiterers and four boot makers/ boot repairers (the most well-known being Sam Brown around in Canterbury Road). There were also two drapers or haberdashery shops. The larger of these was Dowsett's (1911–1960) on the corner of Richardson Street which comprised a big double shop for women at the front and, at the back, a men's store. The smaller drapers was Millers' (1938–1973) which also stocked items suitable for gifts. There was also an Adams' cake shop, a fishmonger, an ironmonger, a dry cleaners, a dressmaker, a newsagent, a post office, a garage, and several banks.

Interior of Millers' Drapery in Armstrong Street, Mrs Beatrice Miller (right) with her daughter Mrs Connie Harvison, c. 1960s

Armstrong Street shopping strip looking north c. 1920–1939

There were also several dairy produce shops, later known as delicatessens, or locally, as 'ham and beef' shops. One at no. 30 Armstrong Street is particularly interesting as it was run by the Flemming family from 1925–1954 – their granddaughter, Jane, became an Olympic track and field athlete and also won two gold medals at the 1990 Commonwealth Games in the long jump and heptathlon. After the Flemming family left, the shop was run by the Estraich family, one of the early post-war European immigrant families who introduced such things as German sausage to the palate of the Middle Park resident.

Above: Armstrong Street shops between Canterbury Place and Canterbury Road 1974

Left: Former Moran & Cato store (on the right) in Canterbury Road 1974

The grocery store 'chains'

In the early 1900s a new type of grocery store began to appear. It was a larger store than those that preceded it and generally was part of a grocery store chain. The earliest of these in Middle Park was Moran & Cato whose shop at 110 Canterbury Road opened in 1914. The type and range of grocery goods available were fairly standard so price became an important factor for the housewife making purchasing decisions. The chain grocery store was able to make use of its centralised buying power to purchase goods at wholesale prices and offered limited self-service to reduce staff costs. Moran & Cato also had 'cash trading only' and this enabled them to offer goods cheaper than if they had to buy and sell on credit. The housewife could also inspect the goods, prices clearly marked, without feeling the pressure to buy. The downside was that there was limited service and no deliveries. Moran & Cato traded for more than 40 years before it closed in 1959. Another of the successful chain grocery stores was Crofts, founded by Arthur (Archie) Crofts, which opened its first shop in 1905 at 73 Park Street, South Melbourne. Their store in Armstrong Street, Middle Park, opened in 1933, initially at no. 15 and then moved to no. 19. In March 1951 Crofts' Stores claimed to be the first self-service grocery store in Victoria when they converted their Northcote store to self-service. It is not known when the Armstrong Street store became self-service but an advertisement appeared in the *Record* in August 1953 proclaiming a big opening sale at the newly modernised Crofts' Self-Service store in Albert Park. In the same advertisement it mentions their other modern stores in Middle Park and Port Melbourne. Crofts became Nancarrows' Self Service in 1971 and extended to take in no. 21. Today we know it as the Middle Park IGA Supermarket.

Tom Cairns, in his account 'Grocer boy: Middle Park 1933–1939' tells of his time working at Crofts during the depression and records that 'The store was not very big with a frontage of only five metres onto Armstrong Street. Floor to ceiling shelving was filled with tins of spices, racks of tinned biscuits, dried fruit, rice, oatmeal etc., all of which had to be weighed out separately for the customer. Under the counter were kept the main weighed-up items such as flour, white sugar and salt. On the floor stood bags of potatoes and onions.' The size and range of goods were much smaller than that on offer in today's supermarkets but would cover the basic items for the average family and also include soap and soap powders, cheese and butter, eggs and bacon. In contrast to some of the chain grocery stores, Crofts took orders and delivered. Tom Cairns describes how, on Tuesdays, he would hop on his bike and collect orders from about forty housewives in Middle Park. These orders were usually written out beforehand but Tom would suggest other items or the weekly special to increase the order. Once he had returned to the shop, the orders would be made up ready for delivery on Wednesday by the driver on his flat-tray, one-horse cart. Smaller orders would be delivered daily by bike.

However, the housewife was not limited to these two chain grocery stores – there were many other smaller grocers who operated in the streets of Middle Park in what we now call 'the corner shop' (often just the front room of a dwelling) and which were in easy walking distance of her home. These smaller grocers relied on providing service – bacon was sliced according to the housewife's specifications, butter and sugar were weighed out. But conversion to self-service for groceries in the 1950s and the availability of pre-packaged goods saw the rapid decline of the grocer as an expert. However, the most dramatic changes in shopping habits came in the late 1950s in the wake of the motor car and following the introduction of television. This decline became final once the large suburban shopping centres began to open in the 1960s and the local grocer was unable to compete on price and expedience.

The newer shopping centres in the (then) outer suburbs provided a great range of facilities. Chadstone (which included a Myer department store) was opened in the 1960s. By the 1970s the shopping centres had a mix of shops such as a department store, a supermarket, and a range of small shops. The now mobile housewife was able to purchase all her family's needs in one weekly trip and store them in her new refrigerator (94% of Australian households had a refrigerator in 1964). Without a body of regular captive customers ensuring their viability, the suburban shopping strips lost business to the shopping centres and once-busy shopping streets became dowdy and half-deserted.

The move of young professionals into Middle Park in the early 1970s may have helped in the demise of the corner store and the local butcher, baker and grocer. The newer type of Middle Park housewife would have had a car at her disposal and would have preferred to do her shopping at a supermarket where she could buy everything, already packaged, in one go, rather than shop locally at individual shops, waiting in line whilst the butcher carved the meat from the carcass or the grocer sliced the ham and bacon.

The shopping strips of Middle Park

There were three smaller shopping strips in Middle Park – two in Mills Street and one in Hambleton Street. The two smaller shopping strips in Mills Street (between Herbert and Hambleton Streets and Little Page and Danks Streets) were able to provide the basic daily needs for the Middle Park housewives who lived in the western sector of the suburb – hairdresser, cake shop, fishmonger, confectioner, dairy produce, chemist, fruiterer, butcher, grocer, boot repairer and newsagent. Today the Middle Park Shopping Centre can still provide the basic daily needs of the local residents, but the Mills Street shopping strips have almost completely disappeared as providers of essential food items with only a milk bar on the corner of Danks Street selling basic groceries.

The third small, but thriving, shopping strip in Middle Park was known as the Hambleton Street shops. This was a group of seven shops on the north-east side of Hambleton Street between Harold Street and Canterbury Place. They were a disparate group of buildings then, dating mainly from the 1890s, but if you looked at them today you would never guess that they had once been shops. They attracted shoppers due the popularity of two of their shops in particular: Baileys' the butcher at no. 113; and Cunninghams' the licensed grocer and later wine and spirits shop, which had the added advantage of a drive-through arrangement at the rear in Canterbury Place. When Baileys was converted into a dwelling, the front window was changed and an entrance made off Hambleton Street – formerly this had been at the back off Erskine Street and was used by the family to access their dwelling which was over the shop. The licensed grocer on the corner was converted into two

Hambleton Street shops 1974 (top) and 2016 (bottom)

townhouses in the 1990s and a second storey added to no. 111 to match the style of no. 109. To complete this set of self-contained shops there was a grocer at no. 115, a Chinese laundry at no. 117, a bootmaker at no. 119, a confectioner at no. 121 and a fruiterer at no. 123. Although the last four of these shops ceased trading in the 1940s the other three remained as shops until the 1980s. So popular was this small group of shops that the South Melbourne City Council engineers department designed and installed an attractive garden-setting bicycle rack outside the shops in the mid 1970s to accommodate seven bikes. They are still there today as a reminder of a lost era of shopping.

Corner shops

The 'corner shop', which also includes mid-block shops, played an important role in the day-to-day life of the Middle Park housewife. Despite the relative proximity of the three strips of shops and the main Armstrong Street shops, the corner shop was usually much closer and the housewife could develop a good relationship with the local shopkeeper who, over time, came to know her preferences. And any last minute shopping needs could be fulfilled by sending one of her children on the errand knowing that the shopkeeper would know exactly what she wanted. The most common corner shops were the grocer, the butcher, the fruiterer, the confectioner, the bootmaker, and the dairy produce store. There were once about forty 'corner shops' in Middle Park, many still operating in the early 1970s and a few into the 1990s. Today there are no corner shops left as they have all have been converted into dwellings.

However the evidence of their former life still remains and can be seen in either the angled wall which once contained an entrance door when the shop was on a corner or in a room that juts out from the front of the house and that was used as the shop. The City of Port Phillip has tried to ensure that these heritage facades remain when the former shop is converted into a dwelling. Two notable exceptions are the former pastry shop/bakery at 94 Mills Street whose façade has been demolished and the former milk bar at 34 Wright Street (now 87 Hambleton Street) whose façade fell over during construction of the two modern dwellings and the developers were required to construct a sham front to indicate its former life as a corner shop.

193 Richardson Street c. 1911–1914

92 Mills Street c. 1913–1919

94 Mills Street 1974 (The shopfront has since been demolished.)

34 Wright Street 1974 (The shopfront has now been replaced by a sham front.)

The butcher, the fishmonger and the greengrocer

A snap-shot from 1940 reveals there were twelve butchers, thirteen fruiterers/greengrocers and three fishmongers operating in Middle Park. By 1974 there were only six butcher shops, six fruiterers/greengrocers and one fishmonger (also the local fish and chip shop). Today (2016) there are none. Except for those who have access to one of the markets or who live in the inner suburbs that still have a butcher, fishmonger and greengrocer, most Melburnians today would buy their fresh meat, fish and fruit and vegetables from the supermarket. And whilst it is still possible to select your own fruit and vegetables, meat and fish are pre-packaged.

One of the longest continuously operating butchers' shops was at 111–113 Hambleton Street, which began as a butcher in 1900. From 1907–1916 the owner was W. Cazaly, an uncle of the famous footballer, Roy Cazaly, who worked there in his youth when footballers were not paid. The shop was then taken over in 1917 by Edgar Bailey, joined later by his two sons, Norman and George, and it remained in the family until it closed on Saturday, 1 October 1983.

When Edgar Bailey started his shop he used a pony and jinker to deliver the meat. Later, George Bailey used a bike with a wire basket on the front and then a Ford car was purchased for deliveries. Baileys had a big truck for bringing meat back from the abattoirs – these were the whole carcasses that were broken down in the shop after hanging on rails. They had a very big refrigerator that all the meat went into because they believed in hanging it for a while. Up until the end Baileys was a traditional butcher, with sawdust on the floor (cleaned and replaced with fresh sawdust three times a week), carcasses hanging on hooks along the rear wall and an enormous wooden block where the meat was cut to the customer's requirements, there being no window display. Before refrigeration, ice was delivered daily and out the back are the remains of stables where the horses and carts were kept for delivery.

George Bailey at the window of his shop and inside at the cutting block 1983.

Another well-known and well-patronised butcher shop was Watkins in Armstrong Street. Fred Watkins began his butchery business in Clarendon Street, Emerald Hill, in the 1860s, later moving to Moray Street. When he retired in 1879 his son, George, took over the business and extended it into the suburbs, opening a butcher shop at 10 Armstrong Street in 1892, then adding another in 1926 at no. 34 in the same street on the corner of Richardson Street. It is hard to imagine a suburb as small as Middle Park supporting so many butchers, let alone two in the same street!

The grocer

The small grocery shop was a staple feature of the corner shops in Middle Park. In 1940 there were twenty-two grocery shops in Middle Park of which thirteen were corner shops and their even distribution meant that the housewife only had a short distance to walk to purchase items she needed. In her oral interview (on the Middle Park History Group website www.middleparkhistory. org) Pat Ness talks about her parents' shop in the 1950s at 42a Langridge Street.

'Our shop was a typical mixed business of the 1950s. It had a milk licence and this was a big part of its success. A lane down at the side of the business made it easy for milk deliveries. Dad was quite a good entrepreneur, and he built up the business. He installed big refrigerators for frozen vegetables and meat, and of course ice-cream was a big seller. He also sold a full variety of sliced meats, many of which he prepared himself on the premises. He never sold fruit or vegetables, as he didn't want to compete with Paddy Walsh around in Park Road, who had the greengrocers' business.'

42A Langridge Street 1974

A very popular and well-patronised grocer was Cunninghams on the corner of Hambleton and Harold Streets and part of the Hambleton Street shopping strip. Les Mowat, in his oral interview, gives an excellent description which also reflects the close community life of the time: '[They] were a family shop, if you wanted cheese, say, they would take a big lump of cheese and cut a slice off… they were a grocer's shop in those days where you had to be served. The biscuits were in tins and they would put some in a paper bag and it used to take a while to get everything, depending on how much talking and gossip you wanted to do.'

By 1974 there were only nine grocery shops left in Middle Park and and whilst the products they once stocked are still available from the local supermarket or the new Gum Tree Food Store, these are both in Armstrong Street and not 'just around the corner'.

Typical interior of a grocer's shop c. 1913–1916

Former grocer's shop 1974 and 2016 at 13 McGregor Street
(corner Richardson Street)

21

Former grocer's shop at 111 Wright Street, 1974 and 2013

The confectioner

Today we would be horrified at the number of 'lolly' shops that existed in Middle Park, most of which were 'corner shops' and mostly serving the needs of children. Whilst the adverse effects of sugar on teeth were well-known before and after World War II, its effect on obesity was not. There were eighteen confectioners in Middle Park in 1940, and this does not include confectionery that was available from the grocer. Of these, ten were 'corner shops'. The most popular 'lolly shop', as they were known to the local children, was the one opposite the Middle Park Central School on the corner of Richardson and Wright Streets and which children would pass on their way home. But there were many more to tempt a child and most were in easy reach of home. So why were lolly shops so popular then with children? In the days when pocket money didn't go very far (because it was never very much), lollies could be purchased for just a few pennies. Toni Risson from the University of Queensland sums it up when she writes: 'For many, buying lollies was our first purchasing decision. As proverbial kids in candy stores, we had to decide whether it was better value to buy one Kit Kat or five Rainbow Balls, a packet of Chocolate Cigarettes or six Musk Sticks, for our pocket money. Buying lollies taught us about value, how to weigh things up and make the right decision.' Risson says, 'The microcosm of an economy is played out through kids and their lollies.' (*Sydney Morning Herald*, 29 January 2013). The typical confectionery shop had large jars, full of lollies, on the counter. After school hordes of children would cram into the shop to select from a range of lollies for their one, two or three pennies. Some of the lollies of the time, many still available today but sold only in packets, included:

- Licorice allsorts – squares of sugar paste between squares of licorice
- Musk sticks
- Licorice straps
- Sherbet bombs – small bags of sherbet with a straw to suck the sherbet
- Gob stoppers – also called rainbow balls because they changed colour as they were sucked
- Chocolate buttons
- Chocolate freckles
- Chocolate bullets – short thin pieces of licorice covered in chocolate
- Toffee apples
- Jelly babies and jelly snakes
- Jubes – softer than snakes and coated in sugar
- Clinkers – a hard brittle confection either pink or yellow covered in chocolate about the size of a fishing line sinker, hence the name
- Mint leaves – green leaf-shaped jelly covered in powdered sugar
- Mint Patti – large round chocolate covered pattie with a soft marshmallow mint centre. They came wrapped in foil
- Bananas – bright yellow and shaped and tasting like a banana
- Jersey caramels – two squares of soft brown caramel joined by a white confection
- Sour worms – like jelly snakes but coated with sour sugar crystals
- Acid drops – sour-tasting lemon, orange and lime rounds of hardened sugar

- Redskins – raspberry flavoured chewy lolly – the original Redskins wrapping featured an indigenous American with a bright-red face in a full feather head-dress, but that disappeared long ago!
- White Knights – a chewy white mint-flavoured rectangular bar covered in chocolate
- Snowballs – large marshmallow balls covered in chocolate and coconut
- Fags – packets of lolly cigarettes
- Jersey toffees – chewy toffee in a cardboard packet divided into small squares of about 6 or 8 toffees, about 6d each
- Cobbers – chocolate covered caramel squares, hard and chewy
- Choo-Choo Bars – hardened black licorice bars that could make your tongue and teeth black after prolonged sucking.

This list does not include cardboard packets of Jaffas, Fantails, Minties or larger confection bars such as Violet Crumbles and Polly Waffles which were more expensive and were mostly bought to take to the cinema on Saturday afternoon.

The demise of the confectionery shop occurred at the same time as the rise of the supermarket where packaged lollies, hanging from hooks in the lolly aisle, were more cost effective. Of the ten confectionery shops remaining in 1974, now called milk bars, only two remain – 23 Armstrong Street and 163 Mills Street. On the next page is an example of a former milk bar on the corner of Kerferd Road and Mills Street which has been converted into a dwelling with no trace of its former life visible from the outside.

*Former
confectioner/
milk bar 111
Kerferd Road
1974 and
2016*

Bread, cakes and pastry goods

Bread has always been a staple part of our diet but no more so than last century when bread was toasted for breakfast, made into sandwiches for lunch, and used to accompany the evening meal. But whereas today (in 2016) we are offered a choice of artisan breads, back then a white loaf of bread was the only choice. There were two bakeries in Middle Park, both baking on the premises and delivering daily to households:

- 18 Armstrong Street, on the island of land between Erskine Street and Canterbury Place. Operating as a bakery from 1890 it was purchased by Patrick Esmonde in 1903 then sold to T.R. O'Connor in 1928. It remained a bakery until 1961.

- 44 Nimmo Street OR 254-256 Richardson Street, now the Middle Park Community Centre. The original baker was Coppard Bros until 1925 when it became Gillespie's Bakery. The bakery closed in 1941 but the grandson of Ron Gillespie, Roger Gillespie, founded Baker's Delight. The building contained the bakehouse, stables, and lofts, with a shop on the corner. The pre-school now occupies the site of the original stables and the branch library is built into the former corner shop. A large and a small meeting hall on the first floor are built into the old flour loft but the four baking ovens on the ground floor have been demolished.

These bakeries not only baked bread, but also made pies and cakes which could be purchased from their shop or from one of the speciality pastry shops (also called bakers) in Mills Street, Armstrong Street or Richardson Street. In her oral interview, Gwen McDonald recalls: 'On the corner of Richardson and

Mills Streets was a bakery specialising in old-fashioned goodies like "matchsticks" [two long rectangles of puff pastry filled with berry jam and cream] and from which quarter Boston buns filled with mock cream could be bought.' (Lorraine Reeves and Gwen McDonald). And in 1944 the *Record* wrote about the retirement of Mrs Flavell who had 'conducted a successful home-made cake shop in Armstrong Street, Middle Park, for several years'.

The demise of these two bakeries was probably due to the rise of the supermarket which stocked pre-sliced, pre-packaged bread baked by the larger bakeries. Today we see a resurgence of speciality bakeries with an emphasis on artisan loaves, but none are baked in Middle Park.

Esmonde's Bakery

Gillespie's Bakery, now the Middle Park Community Centre

Chemists

There were three chemists in Middle Park in the early 1900s – one in Mills Street, one in Armstrong Street and the largest one on the corner of Armstrong Street and Canterbury Road run by A.H. Adler from 1924–1969. A common feature of these early chemists was the window display featuring decorative containers. Inside, the retail area, which was open to the public, was where the patent and proprietary medicines, cosmetics, baby items, cameras and gifts were on display for purchase. To the rear of the shop was the dispensary for the preparation of prescriptions by the pharmacist.

'Chemists compounded and dispensed all their own medications, and pills were counted and put into bottles. The doctors had their own formulas which would be made up by the chemist. Some formulae required the addition of cocaine which was kept in the safe. Other products which would not be seen today included Amyl Nitrate [often used today as a recreational drug], APCs [aspirin, phenacetin, and caffeine], Bex Powders and Vincent's Powders. [The last two were powdered aspirin which came in folded paper packets, the contents of which you tapped onto your tongue and washed down with water]. Ten per cent of the chemist's work was made up of compounding and the rest of counting tablets into jars. Unlike pharmacists today, little advice was given by them.' – oral interview with Lorraine Reeves and Gwen McDonald

Chemist shops still play a vital role in our lives but their number has declined and prescription drugs are pre-packaged. Today only one chemist remains in Middle Park, in the Armstrong Street shopping strip.

Laundries

Following the Great Depression of the 1890s, many Chinese immigrants who had been cabinet makers found themselves out of work and turned to running laundries in Melbourne's suburbs. There were three Chinese laundries in the early 1900s in Middle Park, operating out of fairly small premises – one in Armstrong Street, one in Canterbury Road and one in Hambleton Street. Their clients would have included landladies running boarding houses, single men needing their cuffs, collars and shirts washed or owners of the grand houses in Middle Park who could afford to send their washing out. Occasionally the Middle Park housewife would have used one of the Chinese laundries but she mostly had to contend with a copper in the back-yard laundry, initially heated by wood or coal and later by a gas flame, and maybe also a hand-operated wringer/mangle. With houses becoming connected to electricity and the arrival in 1935 of the electric washing machine, she could have then upgraded to a single or twin-tub electric washing machine which had the advantage of being relatively inexpensive and taking up little room – an important consideration in the small houses of Middle Park. The need to use the local laundry declined and by the 1960s the Chinese laundries had either closed or had become dry cleaners.

Former Chinese laundries –
86 Canterbury Road (left)
and 117 Hambleton Street
(overleaf)

Wood and coal yards

A dominant feature of the Middle Park streetscape is the chimney. Most of the remaining Victorian/Federation/Edwardian houses that make up the suburb today still have at least one chimney, even if it is no longer a functioning one, because an open fireplace was the only form of heating when the houses were built. Wood and coal yards supplied fuel for the open fires and also briquettes for hot water systems. Kath Scanlan, in her oral interview, describes what it was like when open fires were the only source of heating. 'The house in Harold Street was warmed by one fireplace in the dining room. The fire would roar away, you would be boiling on one side and cold on the other. There were quite a few wood yards around the suburb. Wood would be delivered, and Dad would chop it up. One of us would have the task of cleaning out the fireplace.'

In Middle Park there were five major wood yards operating in the early twentieth century, delivering fuel to the local residents. But competition from gas encroached into their business with the formation of The South Melbourne Gas Company in 1873. By 1910 gas ovens and gas hot water systems had become commonplace. Then, in the 1920s, gas fires for living spaces appeared, though they had to compete with the 'cheerful glow' given out by an open fire. But convenience won out and by the end of the 1940s, gas fires were being advertised for their instant cosy heat and the use of an open fire was phased out. Three of the wood yards had closed by the end of the 1930s and the last continuously operating one, at 5 Harold Street, closed in 1971 after opening in 1886. The closure of these wood yards led to the release of large parcels of land in Middle Park and many of the art deco flats that dot the suburb are located where the former wood yards once were.

THE ÆRATED BREAD FACTORY,

38 ARMSTRONG STREET, MIDDLE PARK.

LUNCHEON, TEAS, CATERING.

HOME-MADE CAKES AND PASTRY A SPECIALTY.
FRESH CONFECTIONERY IN STOCK.

RING UP TELEPHONE 1216 WINDSOR.

You will communicate with —

W. H. CAZALY,

CASH BUTCHER,

113 HAMBLETON ST., MIDDLE PARK.

ONLY ONE QUALITY : THE BEST.

Small Goods Fresh Daily.   Sausages and Corned Beef a Speciality.

L. A. MONK,

CYCLE BUILDER AND BRAZING EXPERT,

40 Armstrong St., Middle Park.

BUILDER OF THE "WING" CYCLE.

WORKMANSHIP GUARANTEED.
NEW CYCLES FROM £9 UPWARDS.
ALL ACCESSORIES IN STOCK.

DAIRIES, MANUFACTURING AND OTHER LIGHT INDUSTRIES

Dairies by Diana Phoenix

Manufacturing and Other Light Industries by Sonya Cameron

Middle Park now is a suburb consisting mainly of houses and apartment blocks, with a couple of shopping strips to service the immediate needs of its residents. It is hard to imagine that once there were five dairies and many thriving small manufacturing businesses, many tucked away in back streets and laneways. Some of the buildings of these former industries have been converted into dwellings, others have been demolished and replaced by apartments or modern townhouses. These industries did not necessarily service the local area (though the dairies did), but were probably located in Middle Park because it was on the train line and it was close to the city.

Dairies

Not so long ago in Middle Park, milk was delivered each morning by horse and cart. It was ladled out by the milkman into a waiting receptacle left on the doorstep. Some residents preferred to call at a dairy, jug or billy can in hand.

Supplying milk for the suburb had begun when cattle were allowed to graze in the Albert Park in the mid-19th century, and the cows could provide milk for the nearby residents. At that time it did seem that the animals were locked up at night.

As the population increased so did the demand for milk but there was opposition from the Emerald Hill Council which wanted livestock numbers reduced so that young trees could grow in the park without being damaged. Charges were gradually introduced for grazing. By 1907 an owner was obliged to pay one shilling and sixpence per cow to the Board of Works. However, the following year South Melbourne Council put an end to the keeping of cows for dairying purposes within the city.

When the Health Officer, Dr Daish, submitted his annual report to the South Melbourne Council in March 1900, he stated that 'our dairies are generally very cleanly kept, but the time is now ripe for a proper supervision of all herds supplying the city, and for their periodic testing of tuberculin, and also for the abolition of the small dairy shops which have no accommodation for the storage of milk for even a few hours. Whether cows should be allowed at all in the city is debatable. At all events they should be carefully prevented from drinking from the street gutters or feeding at any rubbish tips'.

Later that year a correspondent writing to the Editor of the *Record* complained of the grazing of cattle and horses in the streets, especially after dark, stating that 'it is hardly safe to walk out at night for fear of coming to grief over some stray animal lying about. Perhaps the present officers have not sufficient time to visit Albert Park and Middle Park or they might see for themselves. If they are not supposed to be out at night the Council might put a man on night duty'. Two years later, in March 1902, the committee in control of the park paid an official visit of inspection there in answer to complaints of residents that they were practically deprived of the use of the place as a park owing to the fact that it was overcrowded with cows.

The report of the municipal Health Officer in 1905 explained that there was a rigid examination of the interiors of dairies to prove that they had a coating of lime, while shops had to store the milk in perforated zinc safes. However, that year the Government proposed to bring a Milk Supervision Bill before Parliament in order to legislate for Government control of dairies instead of municipal supervision. By 1908 annual registration of dairies was in force. Milk was selling at 5 pence a quart. At a meeting of the Melbourne & Suburban Retail Master Dairymen's Association, of which J. Morris was President, a shortage of milk supply was discussed. It seemed that some farmers were sending their milk to creameries in the country rather than supplying the Melbourne milk trade. One farmer present stated that 'girls would get into mischief if not working the separator'.

By 1910 there were five separate dairies operating in Middle Park originating as:

- 10 Herbert Street, later located at 24 Herbert Street, named Hambleton Dairy, owner Martin Dobeli.
- 23 Boyd Street, owner William Gelling.
- 103 Hambleton Street and 86 Carter Street, named Seaford Dairy or Parkdale Dairy or, later, Farnsworth's Dairy, owner H.C. Howell.

- 337 Danks Street, named Bracklyn Dairy, owner Richard Mulligan.

- 45–47 Patterson Street, owner Isaac Thyer, address either Patterson Street or 42 Langridge Street.

A number of members of the Retail Dairymen's Association inspected the refrigeration plant newly installed at the Hambleton Dairy of Martin Dobeli in Herbert Street on 13 January, 1909. He was praised for the lead he had given in respect to local refrigeration of milk. By the following year the Association was asking for a train to bring milk from the Colac district on Sundays in order to keep up with the increasing need for supply on that day of the week.

The Dairy Produce Act of 1919 enabled gradual co-operation between the Public Health Commission, Railways Department and municipalities. Thus by the 1920s the re-sale of milk from shops became limited to select grocers and confectioners, but excluded greengrocers.

Rail transport was increasing, using ice-louvred trucks. Milk had to be loaded on freight trains bound for Melbourne by 5 am, to be collected at Spencer Street Station by dairymen.

The Victorian Milk Board was formed under State Legislation in 1934 to ensure Government control over quality and price. Approximately 300 dairies were de-licensed and paid out by the Board as part of a milk zoning plan which aimed to stop price-cutting, reduce the number of delivery vehicles and inclusive costs. There were two categories for dairymen: Delivery or House Trade, the latter meaning that distribution took place from the dairyman's property only, no carts being used. In 1937 the *Government Gazette* listed places in Middle Park where milk could be sold or distributed by retail for delivery, giving Martin Dobeli, 24 Herbert Street, and Joseph Farnsworth, 86 Carter Street; or milk to be sold by retail as house trade which were Mrs Feign, 45 Patterson Street, Gilchrist, 23 Boyd Street, Mulligan, 337 Danks Street, and listing milk shops in Middle Park: six in all. The demand for bottled milk was increasing as this item could be bought with other products in a shop. Following this, a number of dairymen had gradually bought other rounds to comply with the economic unit of 175–200 quarts to be sold daily. In some cases parts of individual zones overlapped, resulting in the customers' choice of delivery by either of two dairymen.

By 1948 all milk was to be pasteurised and bottled. However, Martin Dobeli had built a pasteurising plant for his business in 1935. Bottles for milk had been invented in 1884 but it is hard to know when they became commonplace in Middle Park, replacing the billy can left out for the visiting 'milko' in his horse and cart.

Milk bottle from Dobeli's dairy, c. 1950s

The Milkap Factory at 202 Little Page Street was first listed there in 1929 as 'bottle wad' manufacturers, producing cardboard tops for bottles. The change to aluminium tops occurred in the 1940s. Reg Boyd talked of playing in the rubbish tips in Albert Park as a boy at that time. He and his friends would find thousands of unused cardboard tops which they would flick like miniature Frisbees.

In 1958 milk cartons were introduced and by 1975 the 600 ml bottle finally replaced the 1 pint bottle. By this date most suburban dairymen were ceasing deliveries.

Dobeli

Joseph Martin Dobeli was born in Sarmenstorf, Switzerland on 19 February 1852. He migrated to Australia on the sailing ship *Iron Monarch*, disembarking at Adelaide on 12 June 1876. He married Mary Cormack on 4 March 1878 in St Aloysius Church at Seven Hills. Their son Martin was born in Clare on 22 March 1879. Some time in the 1890s the family left South Australia and moved to Melbourne where Joseph Dobeli was employed as a gardener. He lived opposite the St Kilda Cemetery where he was buried following his death on 27 June 1899.

Joseph Martin Dobeli's son, Martin, is first listed in Sands & McDougall's Directory in 1908 as occupying a dairy at 10 Herbert Street, Middle Park. His first entry for that address on the electoral roll is in 1912, where he is described as 'dairyman'. In addition, he and Walter Laycock, fuel dealer, are owners of 24–26 Herbert Street which had stables behind. Dobeli is the occupier. The stables opened into Carter Street, therefore are given that address.

It is obvious that by early 1909 this dairy was well-established, as a long description of the refrigeration plant appeared in the *Record* of 23 January, when a group from the Retail Dairymen's Association met there for a tour of inspection. Mr Dobeli was congratulated on the efficiency of his enterprise which consisted of buildings comprising a cold chamber, ammonia plant, gas engine, a boiler for scalding cans by steam, and preliminary cooling troughs. Tests had shown that temperatures in the cold chamber had increased only 2½ degrees Fahrenheit after a period of sixteen hours. Thus the problem of preserving large quantities of milk was overcome.

Former dairy 24–26 Herbert Street, 1974

Martin Dobeli developed an interest in harness racing and kept some of his race horses in the stables at Carter Street. On 8 December 1931 a fire broke out there behind his house. Seven trotting sulkies, harness, feed and a motor car were destroyed in the blaze. A total of thirteen horses were in the stables at the time but were let out by concerned neighbours, to be rescued later as far away as Port Melbourne.

In 1941 the business was sold to Morris Brothers Union Dairy Pty Ltd, of 370 Montague Street, South Melbourne, a well-established dairy organisation with a second depot in Bay Street, Port Melbourne. Robert Morris became the occupier of the house at no. 10 and the brick and weatherboard stables facing Carter Street. Robert Morris and his brothers James and William had worked as partners since 1893.

Stables in Carter Street, rear of the dairy, 1974 (now townhouses and childcare centre.)

Martin Dobeli died in 1966, however the dairy is listed as being occupied by Morris Brothers in 1957, at 24–26 Herbert Street, and stables at 5 Carter Street. Morris Brothers Union Dairy continued to hold the licence for delivery, but not house trade, selling the last of their horses in 1973 when trucks began servicing their round.

Mulligan

Bracklyn Dairy was located at 337 Danks Street, owned by Richard Michael Mulligan and his wife Mary Agnes Mulligan. The family think the property was purchased circa 1909, and that it was previously owned and the house possibly built by the grandfather of former Premier Jeff Kennett. Richard's grandfather had worked as a dairyman on Bracklyn Estate near the town of Mullingar in County Westmeath in Ireland, good dairy country about 80 kilometres west of Dublin. A brass nameplate showing the word Bracklyn was fixed to the front wall of their Middle Park house, and the name, together with a sketch of a dairy cow, was printed on their customer accounts.

Former Bracklyn Dairy when auctioned in 1998

Shane Mulligan, grandson of Richard and Mary, has shared his family archives and his own memories with us:

Bracklyn Dairy sold milk directly to customers from the house, and also delivered. The house had cobbled laneways down the left-hand side (western) boundary, and along the rear (northern) boundary. Regular and casual customers came on foot through a gate built into a high timber fence in the side laneway and rang a bell at a servery hatch in an alcove built into the side wall, to alert a member of the house to come and serve them. A milk churn was placed in the alcove along with a set of different-sized dippers. Customers brought their own containers and purchased whatever amount of milk they wanted. They came from early in the morning until late in the evening seven days a week.

For other customers further away from Danks Street, milk was delivered using two horse-drawn carts driven by Richard and his brother Joe. The carts carried milk churns and sets of different-sized dippers. The horses knew the 'milk round' as well as their masters and would patiently plod their familiar route around Middle Park. Customers would bring out their own containers, according to their needs. The horses would stop outside the addresses of regulars without any prompting. However, it was a different story when Richard and Joe arrived at their last stop. As soon as the last customer had left the side of the cart they [the horses]would turn for home and set off, arriving before their masters who were obliged to return on foot. The gate where they waited was in a tall brick fence which formed the rear boundary and opened into a small open courtyard. Directly off this and built into the corner of the property were the stables which housed the horses, carts and tackle. Adjacent to the stables on the side laneway was a cool room with very thick walls all painted in bright whitewash, with a small chute through the rear wall to the laneway for delivery of slabs of ice to keep the milk cold. The stables were fitted with doors to keep the horses snug and warm in winter, and were drained to the rear laneway. Both the courtyard and laneway were surfaced with fitted house-bricks laid on their sides. The stables contained three partitioned stalls, plus an area for storage and a workspace. Two of the stalls housed the horses and the third was used for tackle racks. A chest-high brick bin was built into the courtyard wall next to the laneway gate for horse manure. This was used to fertilise a vegetable patch. Any surplus manure was sold to local gardeners.

The work at the dairy was shared by Richard and Mary, their seven children, and Richard's brother, Joe, who lived with them. A daughter, Carmel, was granted a life estate over the house and lived there until her death in 1997. The property went to auction in 1998. Extensive renovations were carried out by the new owners, including the conversion of the old stables, cool room and courtyard area into a garage, with an apartment above.

Shane also remembers hearing of the effects of the Depression of the 1920s and 1930s when numerous customers could not pay their milk bills. By 1938 Richard had retired, possibly for this reason, and the dairy closed shortly after that. No doubt this affected other dairymen and shopkeepers.

Gilchrist

Little evidence has been found concerning this dairy at 23 Boyd Street, on the corner of Little Page Street.

It was set up by William Gelling in 1902. In the 1930s it was owned by Arthur Gilchrist, passing to Blenheim in the 1940s and then to Mrs Roberts who carried on until approximately 1950.

Former dairy, 23 Boyd Street, 2016

Farnsworth

Mrs Ellen Farnsworth ran a dairy at 189 Eastern Road, South Melbourne, listed as early as 1897, named Woodclose Dairy. Her brother, Joseph Richard Farnsworth, set up another in Middle Park at 86 Carter Street, with stables behind, at no. 103 Hambleton Street. It operated under the names Seaford Dairy or Parkdale Dairy.

Pat Berger, Joseph Richard Farnsworth's grandson, relates how milk was collected daily from Spencer Street Station then delivered on the Farnsworth local round, all by horse and cart. People also came to the house by way of a side entrance, to make their purchases directly.

The horses were spelled in Albert Park. At some stage a horse and cart won medals at the Royal Melbourne Show. On one occasion when a horse had bolted, with cart still attached, it had ended up at Kerferd Road pier.

*Horse and cart in Hambleton Street (left) and
horse and dray in Carter Street (right), 1934*

Stables in Hambleton Street, 2015

Les Mowat recalls that someone from Farnsworth's delivered cream separately on Sundays. People took a jar out to his cart, to be filled.

The dairy seems to have ceased operating by 1950, but the derrick, or hoist, used for lifting the feed to the upper storey of the stables remains and is visible to the passer-by in Hambleton Street.

Feign

W.H.Feign operated a dairy from his house on the corner of Patterson and Langridge Streets, sometimes listed as at 45 Patterson Street and sometimes as at 42 Langridge Street. An entrance from Patterson Street gave access to a brick building separate from the house, known as the separator room where a side window could be opened to serve customers. This shows that at some period milk was separated here in order to produce cream. Both milk and cream would have been sold at this window, rather than from the house. Behind this building, beside the lane in Patterson Street, stood a small stable, now converted into a 'Granny flat'.

The first evidence of a dairy is in 1900, occupied by Isaac Thyer, but by 1903 William Feign was established there. From 1918 onwards it is listed under the name of Mrs Mary Feign, and after 1923 as 47 Patterson Street. The last entry for Mrs Feign is in 1939, registered to provide house trade only. The dairy must have ceased operation then.

Separator room at Feign's Dairy, 2016

MANUFACTURING AND OTHER LIGHT INDUSTRIES

Commercial laundries

There were two large commercial laundries in Middle Park (not including the laundry work done by the Convent of the Good Shepherd in Beaconsfield Parade), part of its small light industry/ manufacturing side – Albert Park/Nott's Steam Laundry in Mills Street and Beale's Steam Laundry in Erskine Street.

The Albert Park Steam Laundry was founded by Mr Harry Grey and commenced operation in 1889 in Bevan Street and then moved to larger premises at 4–14 Mills Street in 1901. Following

Mr Grey's death in 1914 it retained its name, only becoming Nott's Steam Laundry in 1950. It closed in the late 1980s after it had been taken over by Princes Laundry whose main laundry premises were in Mentone. Beale's Laundry is listed as being at both 92 Hambleton Street and 71 Erskine Street but is the one parcel of land now occupied by a block of apartments. The laundry was opened in 1905 and the proprietor was Frederick Beale until 1917 when the proprietor became James Shadbolt, until his death in 1937. The laundry closed in 1965.

Albert Park Steam Laundry, 4–14 Mills Street

Both of these commercial laundries were large-scale establishments employing twenty-five to thirty staff. They catered mainly to the needs of hotels, steamers and ships. They used the latest machinery such as steam engines, large boilers and ironing machines, steam mangles, starching machines and drying chests. However, both laundries still catered to the needs of individuals and families. In the 1930s Beale's advertised the use of their Dress Shirt Laundry Service and in the 1950s Nott's was advertising itself as a 'family laundry' which would take care of the entire family weekly wash.

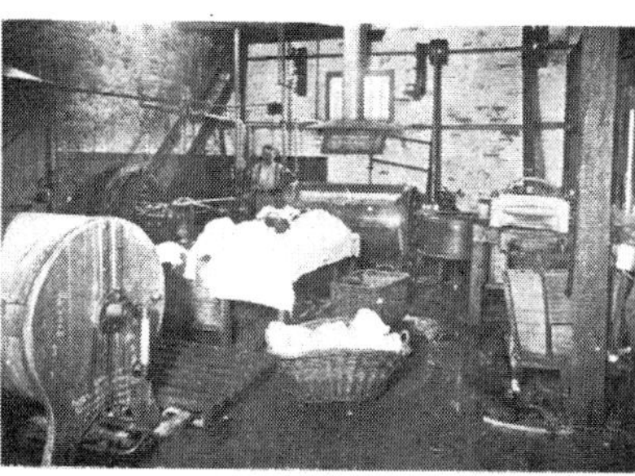

Ironing and washing rooms, Albert Park Steam Laundry, 1905

Manufacturing

At 202–208 Little Page Street, built in 1926, the original occupier of this factory was a button manufacturer but the main occupier was the Australian Seal Company manufacturing milk-bottle tops (initially cardboard circles which were pressed into the neck of the bottle and later aluminium foil caps and crown seals which fitted over the neck of the bottle to seal it). This business was also known as the Milkap Factory and this name appeared on the wall of the factory and remained visible for many years. By the end of 1950 bottle-top production had ceased and the building housed different businesses before being converted into two dwellings.

Former Milkap Factory, 202–208 Little Page Street

At 381–383 Danks Street the Federal Building Material Company, manufacturers of cement tiles, had their premises. The company was established by John Crotty in 1902 as an alternative to slate and clay tiles for roofs. The cement tiles were claimed to be cheap, durable and artistic in appearance and could be manufactured in various colours. The company ceased being listed at this address in 1912 and the land remained vacant until 1937 when the Listowel block of apartments was built.

381–383 Danks Street, site of former Federal Building Material Company, 2016

At no. 36 Patterson Street, from 1902 until 1989, a well-known asbestos factory, Tuck's Asbestos Company, operated out of these premises on the corner of Langridge Street. Before the dangers of asbestos were known, local children played in the white asbestos dust that was blown onto the footpath outside this red-brick building. In her oral interview Pat Ness states that the factory made asbestos gloves and that 'people who worked at the factory were given four pints of milk a day, which was supposed to minimise the risk of asbestosis, as it was thought that the sticky quality of the milk, when consumed, would 'collect' asbestos before it could be digested!' In 1985 Tucks no longer manufactured asbestos there, probably due to the discovery of the dangers of asbestos, and instead the company was known as Tucks' Industrial Packings and also as gasket manufacturers. The factory has now been converted into apartments.

Former Tuck's Asbestos Company, 36 Patterson Street, Middle Park, 2016

Cabinet-maker

A small cabinet-making firm operated out of 74 Little Page Street from 1928 until its closure in 1963 when a fire burned down the factory. In her oral history Lorraine Reeves (nee Clifton) recounts that the factory was a family business started by her husband John's father. He and his brother built a factory behind their house at 265 Danks Street where they carried on the business for many years. John set up a clog-making enterprise in Middle Park with a friend, then later joined the family business. After the factory was burnt down, the site was bought by the Hunters who were wholesalers and needed space for their butter trucks which they operated out of 129 Page Street. There is now a dwelling on the site, behind a red brick wall.

Other factories etc.

Middle Park was once home to two hat manufacturers (Honeybone's Hat Manufacturers and Godfrey Hat Block Company, both in Neville Street) and a net and rope-making enterprise, Oxley's in Langridge Street. These businesses have been written about in more detail in previous Middle Park History Group publications.

There are no dairies, manufacturers or light industries in Middle Park today. The dairies are now dwellings with several still showing traces of former days, such as stables, and one with a free-standing separator room. Of the larger industries, such as laundries, there is little remaining evidence. The light industry premises have gradually been converted into houses and apartment blocks where the casual observer will find the only clue to a busy past is in the size or shape of the building, all in contrast to the surrounding dwellings of varying architectural styles.

SOCIAL CHANGES AND EARLY DEVELOPMENT IN MIDDLE PARK

Max Nankervis

Early surveying and subdivision

The earliest development in South Melbourne or, as it was originally known, Emerald Hill, was in the northern section just south of the Yarra River and across the river from the central 'Hoddle's Grid' laid out (conceptually at least), in 1837. It is in this area that much of the early commerce and industry developed, though in those early days home and business were often combined on the one site. This early subdivision was planned by Robert Hoddle who had very definite ideas on survey and subdivision, in particular that roads should be generally at about one and a half chains (99 feet) wide, and in a grid pattern – a town planning theme which dominated 19th century urban design. This left a very fortunate legacy of wide streets around inner Melbourne, at least until speculators got to work and subdivided, and then subdivided again, producing many small, narrow streets and small sites off the main roads.

Both these factors – Hoddle's wide streets and re-subdivision of sites – later came to affect Middle Park when, and after, it was finally surveyed and subdivided in the 1870s. In part, it was this ever-decreasing size of building sites that helped drive the movement to create Middle Park as a suburb. As the urban development proceeded it had produced cramped and often unsanitary conditions in South Melbourne (and generally in all inner urban areas). The lack of a reticulated sewerage system, which did not come until the 1890s, exacerbated these conditions. Combined with this was the lack of strong building regulations. In particular, Mr Gresswell's 1890 'Report on the sanitary condition and sanitary administration of Melbourne and its suburbs' clearly demonstrated the unsanitary state of affairs.[1]

But by the 1870s there also were many people seeking better urban conditions and who were wealthy enough to aspire to something better, and bigger. The post-Goldrush period of development had produced a somewhat crude built environment. So when the potential of moving to a better environment arose, they were happy and able to take-up the opportunity. The creation of Middle Park was one of those opportunities, and it presented itself on their doorstep. But sitting in the background was another powerful factor; the extraordinary speculative Land Boom which began in the 1870s and gathered steam until the bubble burst about 1890–91.[2] It was this boom, which was interwoven with political chicanery and corruption, that produced enough subdivided land to handle Melbourne's population growth until well into the 20th century. And, incidentally, it brought about a web of suburban train lines which continued to define the shape of Melbourne until the 21st century.

But as well as the 'negative' factors encouraging development in Middle Park there was the 'push' factor. The most recently developed area, that part of South Melbourne generally south west of the railway line south to Kerferd Road (the area generally known as Albert Park), was filling up. Susan Priestley notes the considerable development in that area in the 1870s.[3] So by the late 1870s and early 1880s, Middle Park was an increasingly attractive 'overspill' area.

Land speculation

Thus while the sale and development of Middle Park land was driven, in part, by this boom, unlike in some other suburbs, this was a relatively minor part of the expansion process. Nevertheless, as the boom escalated the plethora of South Melbourne Real Estate Agents in the 1870s (and later) were able to make their mark in selling (and reselling and subdividing) Middle Park. The names of Buxton, Buckhurst, Boyd, Thistlewaite, Swindley, Stead, and Middle Park's very own scoundrel, Matthias Larkin are all connected with intense land speculation. Figure 1 shows the most prolific land buyers of the original 'alienation' sales as the government released sites.

As can be seen, several (speculative) buyers acquired numerous sites over time. Yet, during the ensuing speculative frenzy, some sites must have changed hands several times as the later title holder and eventual developer was a different name.

RANK	NAME	No
1	BOYD D	47
2	BUCKHURST W P	34
3	BUXTON J R	27
4	DURET C	25
5	THICKBOOM J W	15
6	YOUNG J	13
7	FORD A	11
8	VIAL O	11
9	CLARK F	10
10	LEVVY L	10
11	MARTIN W R	10
12	PARKER A	10
13	WAKEFIELD J R	10
14	WRIGHT J R	10
15	LANGTREE O L	9
16	THURGOOD J	9

Figure 1: Top 15 land purchasers at alienation sales, by number of sites

Figure 1 indicates the number of sites attributed to various buyers, but it is worth noting that while D (David) Boyd acquired 47 sites, there are 11 other sites attributed to a Boyd family member. Moreover, the sites were sold in tranches from 1875 until almost all sites were sold by 1925.

While the land boom was essentially driven by private speculators, as Michael Cannon notes, many of the speculators worked their way into the role of parliamentarian, and thus were able to drive the process from the 'driver's seat'. Mr (later Sir) Thomas ('Tommy') Bent is one of the most notorious of these characters, but he was by no means alone in this process. Interestingly, Mr Bent is recorded as the initial purchaser of only one site in Middle Park. But in some ways these very parliamentarians/speculators were driven by an ideological underpinning when they ran the state as their own fiefdom. Thus, when the question of subdividing the 'unused' land between the St Kilda railway line and the beach arose, they had no scruples in subdividing land which, as early as the 1850s, had been set aside as parkland. As Mr James Casey, the Minister for Lands argued in justification for subdividing sites in St Kilda Road in 1875 (out of The Home Park, now Albert Park), he said he was embarrassed that a city the size of Melbourne should have so much open space. In fact, had he got all his own way, another large slice of the park on Fitzroy Street would also have gone the way of subdivision. But such was the protest that he limited his land grab. It could be said that this approach to parkland use has been a consistent theme in relation to Melbourne's parkland.[4]

So by the 1870s, while there were several factors pushing (and pulling) the creation of Middle Park, there were also some restraining factors. Firstly, the land was almost all loose sandy soil, thus not presenting a firm base for foundations, and as well it was in many areas swampy and flood prone. In addition, the Central Board of Health insisted some action be taken on the swamp in the Middle Park area as it presented a health hazard.

Many said of Mr Mouat's development of Montalto in Danks Street, one of the very early owner-residents, that the house would surely sink into the sand.[5] It was this sand and swamp factor which had forced the St Kilda train line, built in 1857, to be raised on a mound for most of its track through the area, and the short-lived branch line from St Kilda to Windsor though the Home Park was built largely on a gantry to avoid the swamp. Moreover, the land was uneven and required extensive (and no doubt expensive) levelling of the sand dunes. Perhaps in recognition of the likelihood of the land being less than highly desirable, or perhaps as a ploy to enhance sales, the sites, once surveyed, were sold off in small lots, though there is a discernible 'pattern' or strategy to the release of sites.

The overall plan of subdivision of the Middle Park area is puzzling. While it generally accords with Hoddle's concept of wide streets, and the 19th century concept of a 'grid' pattern of streets, the grid has its idiosyncrasies, suggesting it was the work of several minds, not all of whom came together in agreement. But notwithstanding that, it is the pattern of land release which is of interest, and which may have partly directed settlement. An analysis of the date of 'alienation' sales (i.e., the first sale of land out of Crown ownership) shows that in many cases every *second* site was sold at any one time, and that 'corner' sites were often sold first. In this way, once actual development occurred on the sold sites, the area would look more 'developed' and thus have greater appeal to later buyers. Figure 2(a) shows a small section of the map listing initial land sales giving date of sale, buyer's name, and dimensions of site. Figure 2(b) sets out the key data in more readable form. Generally the first areas to be available for sale were in the north-east section, around the intersection of Canterbury and Kerferd Roads (initially called Ferrars Street Extension), as well as the area around Armstrong Street and the new Middle Park Station. But despite the potential attractiveness as a 'breath of fresh air', development does appear to be slow to take off after the first sales. It was after all, distant from the centre of business activity (around Clarendon Street), and lacking infrastructure such as metalled roads and good drainage.

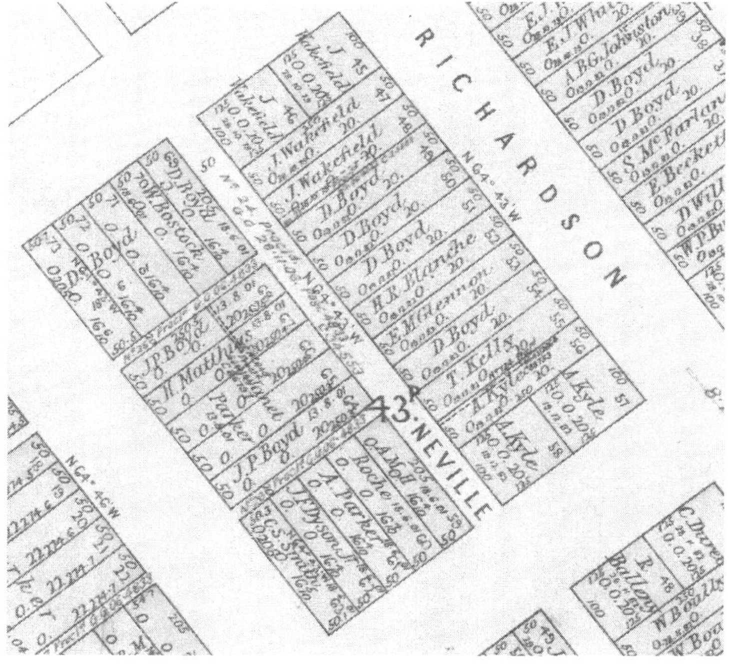

Figure 2(a): Small section of map of initial alienation sales of Middle Park land

WRIGHT ST

RICHAR · NEVILL · PAGE ST

D BOYD	D BOYD	D BOYD	D BOYD	D BOYD
18/06	18/6	18/6	18/6	18/6
1901	1901	1901	1901	1901

LANE

J P BOYD	.13/08/1901
H MATTHEWS	13/08/1901
POWER	13/08/1901
POWER	13/08/1901
J P BOYD	13/08/1901

LANE

C	J	A		A
SMITH	DYSON	PARKER	ROCHE	MOLL
,18/06				18/06
1901				1901

HAROLD St

J WAKEFIELD	J WAKEFIELD
28/10/1979	
J WAKEFIELD	28/10/1873
J WAKEFIELD	28/10/1873
D BOYD	19/12/1882
D BOYD	19/12/1882
D BOYD	19/12/1882
H BLANCHE	
E McGLENNON	
D BOYD	
T KELLY	19/12/1882
A KYLE	19/12.1882
A KYLE	A KYLE
19/12/1882	19/12/1882

Figure 2(b): Data of map 2(a) shown more clearly

But, of course, the speculative land boom did not sit in an economic and social vacuum. The 1870–80s was a period of significant migration to Australia, especially from 'the home countries' (England, Scotland and Ireland) and as well, in many cases the colonies like India. For many Australians, their descendants first arrived in Australia in this period. Such a migration phenomenon put greater pressure on the housing (and associated) markets, and Middle Park was part of the process of reacting to this. While it is not possible to know which new residents were recently arrived migrants, the Sands & McDougall

Directories do note many non-Anglo names of occupiers, indicating that they were perhaps European migrants.

The depression of the 1890s

Another obstacle to development was the terrible depression after 1891 when the frenetic land boom crashed – and several perpetrators went to gaol for fraud. For many who had felt that their investment in property, including land in Middle Park, had made them rich, they suddenly found that the wealth was just a chimera. As some of the sales analysis shows, it was not until after about 1895 that the economy showed signs of recovery, and even then, growth was slow. Earlier the most frenzied location of residential development was in Albert Park, south-west of the railway line towards the beach. As a result, the dominant architecture of that area is distinctly different from that of Middle Park. The former is more Victorian, while the latter is more Edwardian.

Initially development was at the northern end of Canterbury Road and Kerferd Road, but by 1881 the area was still a series of semi-isolated houses, with almost nothing south of Armstrong Street. While it was the common practice of developers to build terrace type houses in pairs or groups, and rarely more than four or five, in the northern section of Canterbury Road most are free-standing, single, houses, with a few pairs – and even fewer triples. This pattern remained until about 1895 when there was considerable 'infill' of sites, though still little beyond Armstrong Street. But by 1905 there was some development south of Armstrong Street, and by 1910 there was some significantly increased activity across the whole area. The southern section remained relatively undeveloped, though by 1915 most Canterbury Road sites had been developed, including the formerly sparsely developed section south of McGregor Street.

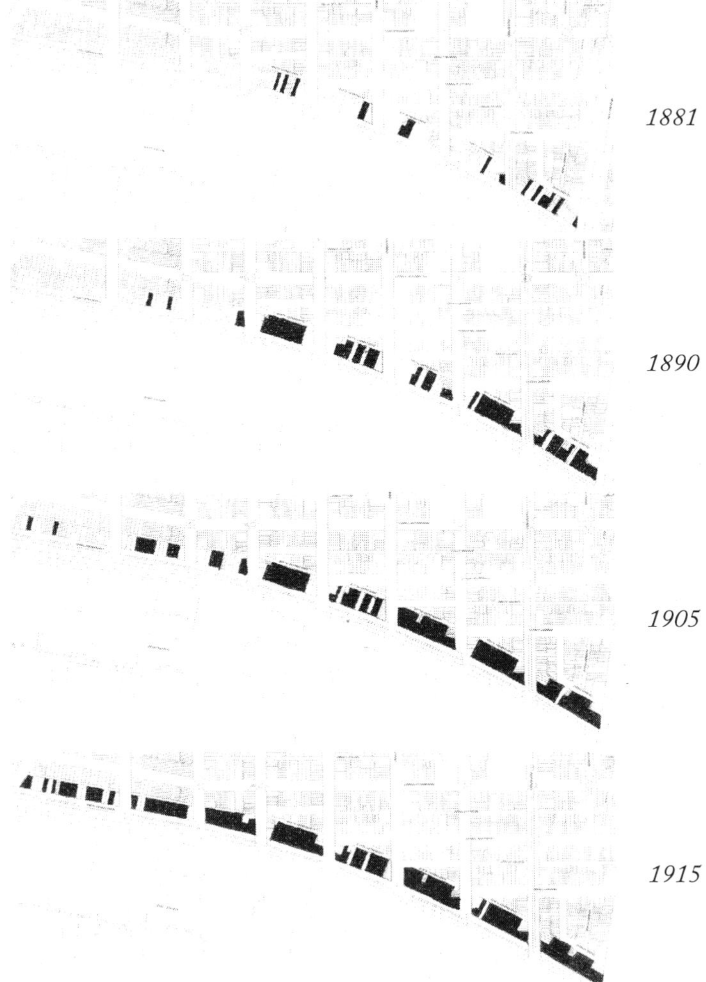

Figure 3: Approximate development of sites, Canterbury Road,
at four points in time: 1881, 1890, 1905, 1915

Uneven development of the suburb

Nevertheless, development was uneven. For example in some streets, one side of the street was heavily developed but not the other side, and overall, streets appeared to develop in an ad-hoc pattern. For example, Beaconsfield Parade was much later than Canterbury Road in density of development, as can be seen in Figure 4. Moreover, there were whole sections of Middle Park where there was no development, and even some maps of the period omit any street layout. The former 'Butts' area around Wright Street is one such area, and some maps show Richardson Street as non-continuous between Mills Street and Kerferd Road.

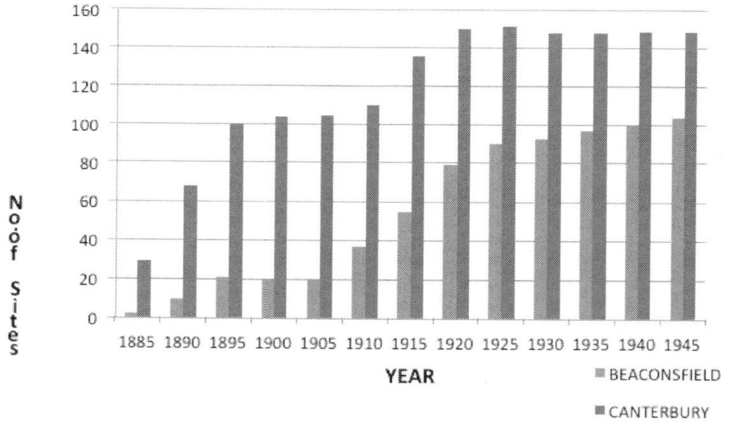

Figure 4: Rate of site development of Canterbury Road and Beaconsfield Parade compared: 1885–1945

It would appear that in those sections which were sold, a pattern of semi-isolated development emerged, though, if anything, the greater the distance from the Canterbury-Kerferd Roads corner, the slower the development. So for many years those early settlers would have found themselves somewhat isolated, and given the reported complaints about the state of the roads and drainage, some might have had second thoughts about their move. Susan Priestley notes that while the area north of Kerferd Road had increasing land prices, the Middle Park area seemed to be languishing by comparison with sites difficult to sell.[6] Even the headmaster of Middle Park State School wrote to the Education Department in July 1888 suggesting that the prospects of increased population (and thus school growth) in the near future were not good, especially due to poor drainage and muddy roads. He seems however, to have been wrong, as four years later the school was requesting another teacher to cope with the numbers which had increased to around 600 pupils.[7] On the other hand, similar to the post-World War II exodus to new suburbs in outer Melbourne where there was space and perhaps even a garden, the new early settlers might also have had some positive feelings about their move. Moreover, it does appear that from its inception, Middle Park did hold some social cachet as a respectable address, especially in comparison with the now somewhat degraded South Melbourne.

One of the notable points about the early residents is their relative parochialism in their residential moves. It is even more the case with the land speculators who bought land, or houses to rent as an investment. These new residents were very often former residents of South Melbourne, and in the case of speculators, almost exclusively so. Very few investment purchasers of rental properties are listed in the Rate Books as having an address in other than South Melbourne, with just a few from country Victoria or interstate. Central Melbourne is the most common alternative address, and generally this was the address of the office of a bank or finance institution, or solicitor. However, some of the key speculators do appear to have moved to live in Middle Park, thereby showing their faith in the emerging suburb. Matthias Larkin and John Buxton are two such examples of land speculators. Thomas Mouat, Samuel Mullen and John Shaw are other wealthy former long-term South Melbourne residents who also built and moved to Middle Park.

Based on an examination of the address of a selection of residents of Canterbury Road, Young Street and McGregor Street in 1890, the current occupier's address was compared with their residential address five years earlier. Twenty-two out of ninety-three (about 23 per cent) names of occupiers can be traced with some reasonable certainty to a South Melbourne address in 1885. In addition, one each came from Port Melbourne and St Kilda, while two each came from Richmond and Collingwood, all suburbs which suffered the same cramped and worn-out ambience and infrastructure. For these people, Middle Park would have offered an attractive alternative and better living conditions. So perhaps locals saw Middle Park in much the same way as inner urban residents of post-war Melbourne perceived a move to suburbs like Mount Waverley and Balwyn – the chance to begin a new suburban life.

Of course, not every one of these new migrants came to own a house in Middle Park, though there were suggestions made in Council that actual home ownership in Middle Park was higher than elsewhere. While this does appear to be the case, there is no clear evidence which compares owner-occupation with similar areas, or Melbourne as a whole. Home ownership as a majority tenure was largely a post-World War II phenomenon, and one which is currently in steep decline. Possibly a majority of houses were owned by investors. A survey of a selection of streets which were developed as residential sites in Middle Park (and it was almost exclusively residential development) indicates that owner-occupiers (which in some cases represents adjoining vacant land) only made up about 38 per cent of the total, although some streets did have a higher ratio of owner-occupiers. But in almost every case, the address of the owners of the investment properties is given as South Melbourne (which could include Middle Park).

Daniel	Maddern	Shipping agent	1
Robert	Balleneuf	Baker	2
Abraham	Barnett	Builder	4
Thomas	Belsen	Gentleman	2
Richard	Burton	Gentleman	2
John	Buxton	Auctioneer	2
Thompson	Ferguson	Gentleman	2
Thomas	Jennings	Grocer	1
James	Kerr	Gentleman	2
Matthias	Larkin & Os	Agent	17

Figure 5: Vacant-land landlords by number of sites owned, Canterbury Road

A suburb of rental properties

One of the notable phenomena of residents' tenures in the mid 19th century is the degree of internal 'migration'. That is, the general brevity of stay at any one address, before moving. Probably underlying this pattern was the fact that so many people were renters, and with probably few or no regulations constraining landlords (or occupiers), and the fact that household possessions were probably relatively few, forced or chosen moves were relatively easy. Nevertheless, there must have been quite a trade in moving, a process which would probably have been effected using horse and dray. Of course, with a higher degree of home ownership, longer periods of length of stay would be expected. Figure 6 shows the average length of stay at an address at three points in time and indicates that over time, residents stayed longer at their address, rising from about 9 to 14 years between 1890 and 1915. A closer inspection of sites in Nimmo Street indicate several cases where the house remained in the family for over thirty years, and in one case more than forty-five years. Consistent with overall gender longevity expectations, very often the listed resident (in Sands & McDougall Directories) switched from a male to a female (Mrs), and in some cases, to what appears to be an offspring, almost certainly following death of a family member.

Street	1890	1895	1915	Average
CANTERBURY	10.2	13.7	16.1	13.3
NIMMO	8.1	7.5	13.4	9.7
HERBERT	9.5	12.9	12.1	11.5
Average(yrs)	9.3	11.4	13.9	

Figure 6: Average length of stay at an address over time. Years 1890, 1895, 1915

Developers, land buyers and builders

The purchasers of the Middle Park sites at the initial 'alienation sales' were quite varied, though as Figure 1 shows, there were some individuals (or family groups) who purchased multiple sites. But as the frenzied land speculation boom proceeded, two other phenomena started to reshape the environment. The first was what must have been a pattern of sales and resales of the land, which enabled the more vigorous speculators to acquire significant tracts of land. One of the most prolific (and corrupt) buyers was Matthias Larkin who acquired several stretches of streets as vacant land, as well as numerous established properties (both in Middle Park and generally around South and Port Melbourne). While the 'occupation' of the land purchases was varied from gentleman to labourer, James Davies of Sandhurst (Bendigo) had no compunction in declaring his reasons for his property holdings, listing his occupation as 'speculator'. Figure 7, a selected page of the 1890 Rate Book, shows just how Larkin, under the name of 'Mathias Larkin and Others' had bought both large adjoining tracts, as well as individual sites.

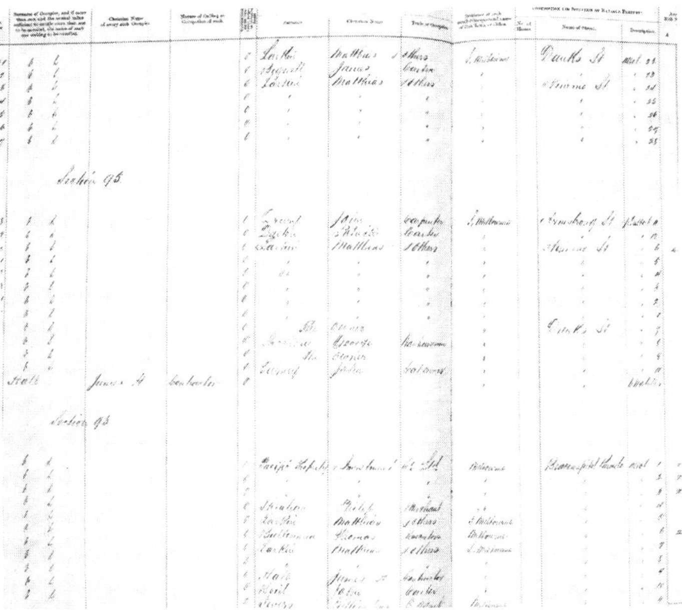

Figure 7: A section of a selected page of the 1890 Rate Book highlighting Matthias Larkin's holdings

But there were others who also bought tracts of land (as well as individual sites). Louis Ah Mouy, one of whose sons was an architect and whose skills were no doubt employed in projects, bought some large sites and appears to have been the developer of several terrace rows. William Druce, whose occupation was listed as 'agent', also bought tracts, as did George Mowling, a 'manufacturer'.

One of the most prolific land buyers and developers was Abraham Barnett who appears to have acquired multiple sites around the north-eastern area such as Mills, Wright, Harold, Nimmo, Hambleton and Carter. But he was a buyer with a purpose. He then went on to develop numerous rows of single-storey, single-fronted, wooden houses in sets of five, six and seven adjoining houses. His style of simple cottages is easily recognisable and those in Figure 8, are typical examples of his single-fronted, single-storey, adjoining wooden cottages.

Figure 8: Current photo of a row of houses built by speculative builder Abraham Barnett. Note: most houses appear to have undergone some form of facade alteration over time

Mr Barnett then appears to have sold several of his cottages and rented out others, even within the same row, such as at 9–13 Wright Street. Possibly the rental period was simply a period of waiting for a buyer. The 1890 Rate Book shows that in some rows of Barnett's terraces there were also vacant houses, suggesting they were just newly built and awaiting a buyer or renter. So busy was Mr Barnett that he appears to have had a site set aside as a workshop or works depot on the corner of Harold Street and Canterbury Road – now a block of 1930s apartments. He also appears to have occupied at one stage the land on the corner opposite his workshop, the site on which Lanark Terrace was eventually built. As well, he owned the sites of some shops in Armstrong Street.

The occupation of the residents of these small cottages, which gives something of a clue to their social status, is very mixed, and there seems no discernible difference between buyers and renters. For example, the occupation (and thus social status) of residents of a row of 16 houses built in Erskine Street (between Wright and Mills) by prolific builder Malcolm Morrison has a wide variation with little correlation between owner and renter, as Figure 9 shows.

	Name		Occupation	Status
1	Joseph	Bullman	Bricklayer	Tenant
2	Thomas	Hornidge	Engineer	Tenant
3	James	Sly	Brushmaker	Tenant
4	Richard	Simpson	Coppersmith	Owner
5	Wiliam	McGregor	Turner	Owner
6	Ernest	Stopp	Baker	Owner
7	Marg	McArthy	Female	Tenant
8	George	Law	Joiner	Tenant
9	George	Fairy	Baker	Tenant
10	David	Quinlan	Carrier	Owner
11	Richard	Bourke	Carpenter	Tenant
12	John	Ramsay	Carpenter	Owner
13	Daniel	Mcnamara	Musician	Owner
14	Anne	Yeoman	Female	Tenant
15	John	friend	Labourer	Tenant
16	John	Mingah	Labourer	Owner

Figure 9: Tenure status and occupation of occupants, houses built by Malcolm Morrison, Erskine Street, 1890

Landlords and renters

But Barnett was not alone in his development zeal, especially of small, single-storey, single-fronted, wooden cottages. Several of the multiple site owners were listed as 'builder', or 'contractor', as was Alexander Lee who owned (and presumably built) numbers 7–13 McGregor Street. Mr Farr, a 'builder' owned several sites in Armstrong Street, and Thomas Clements, also a 'builder', owned sites in Mills, Page and Boyd Streets. John Chard was another somewhat prolific builder of small three- and four-roomed cottages, such as (then numbered)[8] 15–23 Wright Street, as well as 33–41 Carter Street. Joseph Smith, an engineer, who is listed as owner-occupant of number 47 Hambleton Street, owned six, four-roomed, wooden houses in Herbert Place and rented them to: a civil servant, a clerk, a painter, two labourers, and a plasterer. Perhaps of higher social status was William Wells, an architect who owned six four- and five-roomed wooden houses in Young Street.

Then there were the 'small time' investors such as John Tierney, a 'labourer', who owned just one site in Page Street as did James Brodigan, also a 'labourer', who owned just one site in Erskine Street. Women were also sometimes listed as investment property owners. Mrs Elizabeth Harvey, whose occupation, like almost all women was listed as 'home duties', owned 7–21 Nimmo Street, all established houses rented to tenants. This group of houses is of special interest as it is a row comprised of six, single-fronted, single-storey, brick cottages, with a shop at either end on the corners of Erskine Street and Canterbury Place. The shop/house on Canterbury Place is not only double-storey, but slightly wider than the other shops (and houses). Other women are listed as the owner of perhaps two houses, often a 'pair', where they are listed as the occupier of one and landlord of the adjoining house. This was the case for Elizabeth Manson who lived at 31 Herbert Place, but rented out the adjoining number 29, as well as numbers 21 and 23. In some cases the owners of several adjoining sites were listed as family members, such as the Ivers family, all listed as Estate Agents, where William (senior) owned two sites while sons William, James, George and Robert, owned one site each in Beaconsfield Parade.

In some contrast to these small, wooden cottages were the residents of northern Canterbury Road. For example, numbers 15–21 were all owner-occupiers, and the houses are noted as eight- to ten- roomed brick, and residents included two managers, a commissioner, an engineer, an estate agent, a law clerk and a bookmaker. Somewhat surprising is John Boyd, purchaser of several sites over the years, noted as the owner-occupier of number 6 Canterbury Road, a six- roomed, wooden house. Perhaps he intended to demolish and rebuild, for that site is now a single-storey, double-fronted brick house of surprisingly simple design, and architecturally typical of a later period.

Dividing the larger blocks for profit

The other process which came to shape Middle Park was the post-sale subdivision pattern. As can be seen in Figure 2, most sites were originally sold with frontage measurements of 50 links (about 10 metres/33 feet) width, and varying depth from about 100 to 250 links. However, there were various other configurations, including such as those of corner sites (See Figure 2), and also some larger sites fronting Beaconsfield Parade. When the area was surveyed there were criticisms that the sites were too small – perhaps as an over-reaction to the very small sites which had evolved in parts of South Melbourne. Although against this claim it was argued that the wide streets would provide ample 'air' and space.

But some builders, having acquired multiple adjoining sites, re-subdivided to achieve greater gains. And so, many sites in Middle Park emerged with a frontage similar to the older pattern of the inner suburbs. A 50 link site (of approximately 33 feet) could be divided in two, yielding two 25 link (16.5 feet) frontages, a common measurement for a single-fronted, terrace-type house. In other cases two (or more) adjoining sites were re-subdivided into three sites of about 22 feet width, potentially enabling a somewhat larger house. Figure 10 compares the subsequent subdivision of a section of the original subdivision (seen in Figure 2 (a, b) on Richardson/ Wright/Neville Streets, yielding thirty house sites from the original fifteen. However, many sites, especially later developed ones, were developed in their original 50 link width enabling a 'double-fronted' house which would have had significant appeal to those willing and able to pay for such improved amenity.

The residents of early Middle Park

As has been suggested, Middle Park probably attracted people whose circumstances enabled them to choose where they lived, even though they may have been renters. The suburb did appear to be 'modish', as the press sometimes described it. Though it was not as 'modish' as the almost concurrently available sites in Queens Terrace (now Queens Road) where the sites were all large (100 × 200 feet), and with a covenant or regulation that required the houses be substantial.

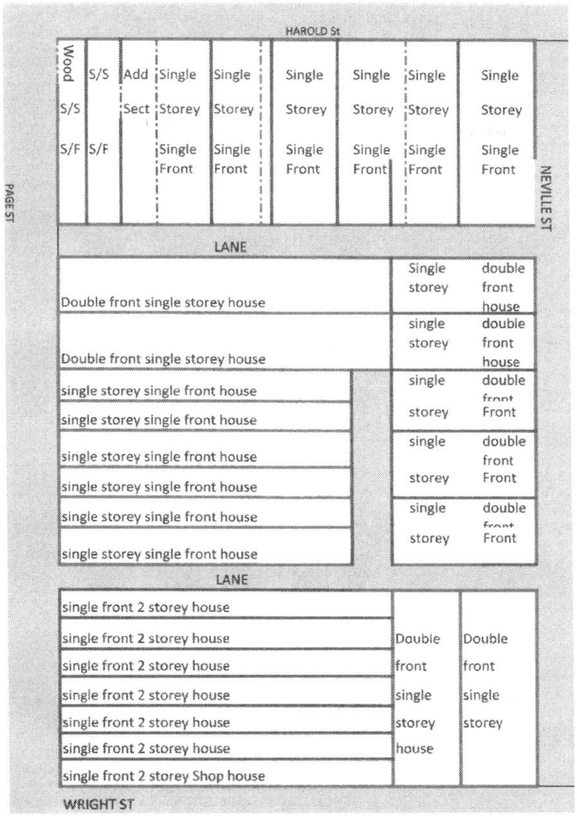

HAROLD St

Wood | S/S | Add Sect | Single Storey | Single Storey | Single Storey | Single Storey | Single Storey | Single Storey
S/S
S/F | S/F | | Single Front | Single Front | Single Front | Single Front | Single Front | Single Front

PAGE ST — NEVILLE ST

LANE

	Single storey	double front house
Double front single storey house		
	single storey	double front house
Double front single storey house		
single storey single front house	single storey	double front Front
single storey single front house		
single storey single front house	single storey	double front Front
single storey single front house		
single storey single front house	single storey	double front Front
single storey single front house		

LANE

single front 2 storey house		
single front 2 storey house	Double	Double
single front 2 storey house	front	front
single front 2 storey house	single	single
single front 2 storey house	storey	storey
single front 2 storey house	house	
single front 2 storey Shop house		

WRIGHT ST

Figure 10: Result of subsequent subdivision section of block, Richardson, Wright, Neville Streets

One interesting unanswered question is what became of those new house-owners, or indeed some of the less wealthy speculators in land and rental houses when the bubble burst on the great land speculation frenzy in about 1890–91. In a short time, it is likely many of these people would have found themselves unemployed and with a mortgage to pay. Did they have to abandon their house, or was it repossessed by the liquidators of the several failed financial institutions? Many of these new owners would have been mortgaged to the South Melbourne Permanent Building Society which it transpired was anything but permanent. Destroyed by the financial chicanery of Matthias Larkin and Patrick Cleary, the liquidators finally moved to repossess many houses around South Melbourne (which would have included Middle Park), in order to pay creditors and stockholders a small dividend. These lower income residents would have been hardest hit, while the 'big end of town' often covered themselves by making secret arrangements with their creditors.[9]

Despite what must have surely been the case, it does appear (based on Sands & McDougall Directories) that there were few completely vacant houses in Middle Park during 1891–1892 when the worst phase of the depression was at hand. Nor are there any strong signs of a change of tenancy suggesting one tenant or resident being moved-out to be replaced by one who can pay the rent. There may have been some cases of landlords agreeing to a reduced (or no) rent for a period, but this would not apply to those owners with a housing loan to pay. This contrasts with Priestley's data which suggests an overall figure of about 9 per cent of houses in South Melbourne vacant at this period, and a significant exodus out of the suburb.[10] Perhaps the Middle Park resident class was on a firmer financial footing than in other parts of Melbourne, including South Melbourne where the Benevolent Society was put under extreme pressure with desperate cases of starving families.[11]

So, who did take up the challenge of living in this new suburb? An analysis of new residents in a selection of streets gives some indication of the 'social class' of those who elected to take-up the challenge. The data for this analysis is derived from two main sources; various years of South Melbourne Rate Books, and Sands & McDougall Directories. While we can assume the Rate Books are generally correct – after all Council's income depended on extracting money from the correct person, the same cannot be said of the Sands & McDougal Directories. They are often wrong, and almost always a year or so out of date. Nevertheless, they together do help build a good picture of the residents.

An analysis was undertaken of the occupation of the land and property owners and occupiers of the houses in a variety of selected streets. The aim was to see if there were any detectable differences in the 'social class' composition by class or style of street. Canterbury Road was selected as it appears to have more substantial houses than nearby Young Street where the houses are somewhat smaller, more often wood, and on smaller sites in a narrower street pavement. Thus it provides a contrast. McGregor and Nimmo Streets are more typical of the architectural style and standard of houses in Middle Park; a mixture of mainly brick single- and double-fronted houses. Figure 11, over the page, shows the percentage of each occupational group of the residents both owners and renters across the selected streets.

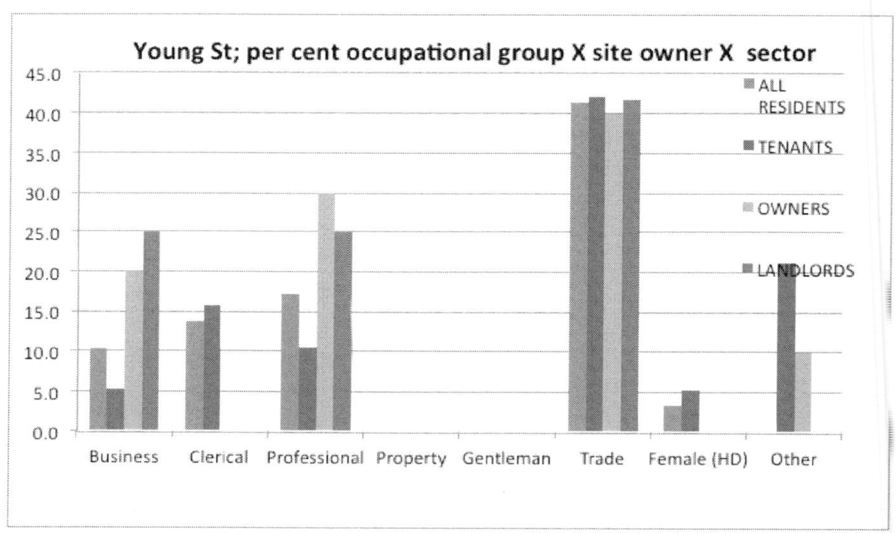

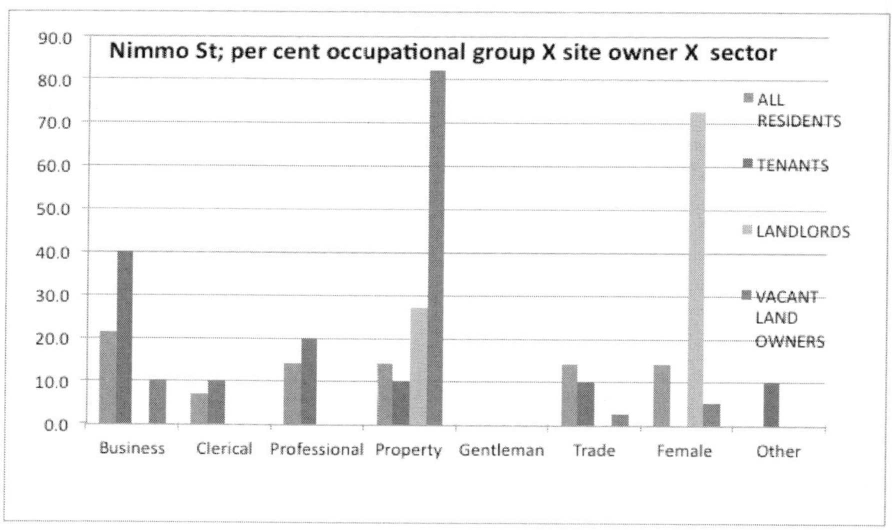

Figure 11: 1890 Occupation of residents, selected streets; per cent of total in each group

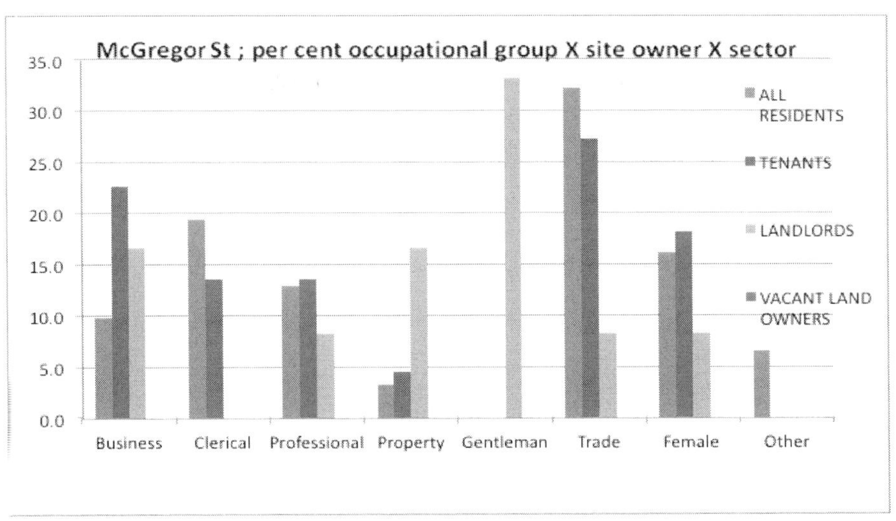

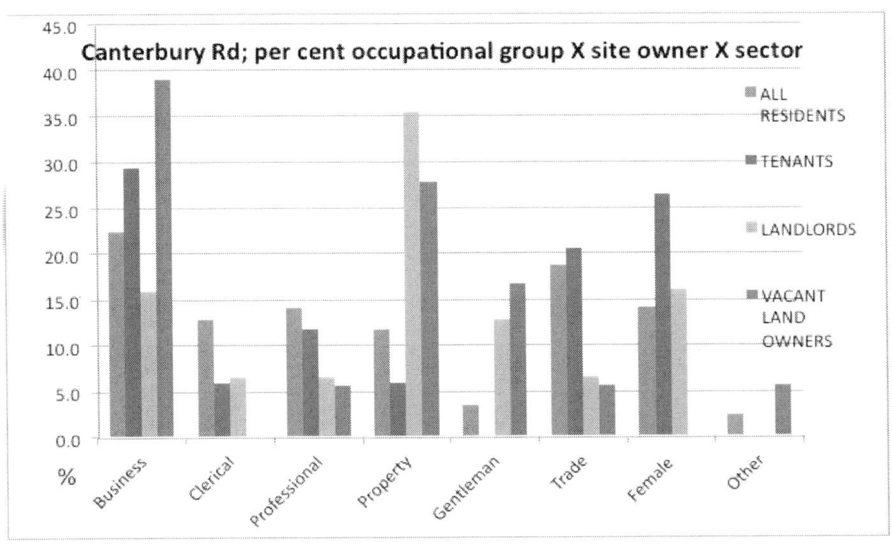

Figure 11 (continued)

A middle class suburb

At this distance of well over a hundred years it is difficult to gauge with accuracy the 'social status' of particular professions or occupations. And, based on the method of analysis and coding used it should be understood that occupations in a particular 'grouping' can vary widely. For example, the 'business' category included those who listed themselves as 'merchant', a nomenclature which appeared to range from a small shop owner to a largish factory owner. 'Gentleman' is another title by which few would wish to be described today, though it did seem to suggest a person of wealth who did not attend a workplace each day. Likewise, 'property' included both builders and real estate agents, both categories of which there were numerous listings. And females included those described as either Mrs or Miss, whose occupation is invariably noted as 'home duties', though one suspects that some of them were in fact in the 'business' of speculating as much as some men. Despite the difficulties of coding, some differences can be discerned by street and occupational grouping.

The overall occupational grouping across Middle Park around 1890 (based on selected streets), at a time when Middle Park was just beginning to grow, and was still very much a 'new' suburb, is widely spread. However, it would appear that the newly settled residents of Middle Park, both owner-occupiers and tenants, were reasonably financially comfortable and skilled in various roles, though by no means a very wealthy group, with a few exceptions.

Occupations

At least 75 per cent of residents appear to have a specific, identifiable occupational role, and even among the 'trade' group (as coded), many of them were more qualified than just 'labourer'. Indeed, the simple designation 'labourer' is relatively rare in the rate lists, even though at that period the economy would have generated a large, unskilled workforce. Wherever those unskilled workers lived, it was not in Middle Park. On the other hand, only about 2 per cent designated themselves as 'gentleman'. The many self-made men of great wealth who would have seen themselves as a 'gentleman', generally established themselves elsewhere, especially in the near eastern suburbs such as Toorak and Caulfield. Despite that a few did select Middle Park as the location of a substantial mansion, Messrs Buxton and Larkin being among those few exceptions. A few others, such as Mr Mountain and Mr Buckhurst moved slightly east to Queens Terrace (Road) or South Yarra. In general, Middle Park was a more 'middle class' suburb than highly prestigious.

Those making up the 'professional' group ranged across accountants, architects, chemists and engineers, as well as 'train driver'. While train driving is not a high-status occupation today, it was one which apparently was well-paid, skilled (driving steam locomotives), and one which endowed the person with considerable responsibility.

'Business' is also well-represented, and included those who described themselves as a 'merchant', as well as those who described themselves in a business such as 'draper'. One suspects that behind the descriptor 'merchant' was a fairly substantial, private business employing several workers, while the drapery was more likely to be a relatively small, single-shop business, often using only family as labour. Nevertheless, owning such a business could lead to a comfortable living. Men such as John Shaw who eventually built 'Somerset' at 224 Danks Street seems to have gained considerable wealth through his drapery store in Clarendon Street, though he also later became an estate agent which may have been a greater wealth generator.

About 13 per cent of the owners and tenants are female, including some designated as 'Miss', though generally 'Mrs'. But these women appear to be either unmarried or widowed, and acting as head of the household and financial controller, and we can assume there was no male as part of the household. As was the protocol of the age, the male would have been listed as head of the household had he been present. Indeed there are several vacant land sites where the rateable owner is listed as a female, so we can assume they were also investors (and speculators) alongside the men. While it is possible others may have been a 'landlady' in a boarding house, it would appear that the pattern of taking in boarders developed later. This female role in property (as landlady) was a continuing one, and over the next several decades many women are listed as head of the household, and in later decades, especially after World War I, they were landladies whose 'job' (and sole income) was managing a boarding house. It was one of the few income-generating roles available to women.

There is also a significant proportion of 'clerical' role residents, who in most cases were listed in the Rate Books as 'CS' – Civil Servant. While we might see many public service jobs today as fairly ordinary, such a job would have had considerable status (and security), and certainly designated a good solid citizen.

The 'trade' group is by far the largest category, though that designation included a wide range of specific roles. Commonly listed was plumber and gas fitter, printer, carter, warehouseman, plumber and plasterer. Another common designation was 'builder', though (in the coding) this was allocated to the 'property' group, but might also have been otherwise designated as trade. At this stage in Middle Park's development, builder (along with 'agent') was a common designation in the Rate Books, more often it was as a vacant land owner than actual resident.

Perhaps the biggest contrast in resident status is between Canterbury Road and Young Street. Canterbury Road was not only home to a considerable group of businessmen, but that group was also extremely highly represented among the vacant land owners, especially for the land south of Armstrong Street. Young Street had only half the proportion. Conversely, Young Street had more than double the proportion of those designated as 'trade'. This difference in occupational status is also evident in the built form as many of the houses in the northern part of Canterbury Road are substantial, terrace-type houses (even where physically separated) on deep, wide sites, while the majority of Young Street houses are single-fronted, wood houses and small sites.

Rogues and gentlemen

Canterbury Road is the only street where 'gentleman' is recorded for actual residents, though McGregor Street has a (small) group of absentee gentleman landowners. And keeping in mind the small number of sites in the sample in the street analysis, McGregor and Nimmo Streets both have a significant group of landowners and landlords as opposed to owner-occupiers.

Of those who owned vacant land in Middle Park, they were commonly owners of multiple sites as Figure 5 shows for Canterbury Road. In particular it shows Matthias Larkin (as 'Matthias Larkin and Others') as the single biggest vacant land-holder, a pattern which was repeated around almost every street in Middle Park. It was this situation which became a dire problem when he was caught and gaoled for fraud in 1892, and the liquidators then found themselves with a massive land portfolio of property to dispose of in a market which had completely collapsed after 1891. But despite Larkin's monopoly on land, the general pattern of vacant land ownership shows a wide variety of occupations among speculators, ranging from a baker and a grocer, to the inevitable property auctioneer, to gentlemen. The pattern of multiple holdings was replicated to a lesser extent in landlords (of houses). Figure 12 shows that three owners dominated the rental market in McGregor Street, with Mr Richard Burton the owner of no less than twelve rental houses.

Richard	Burton	G'man	12
Thomas	Hill	Builder	5
Alexander	Lee	Builder	5

Figure 12: Rental landlords in McGregor Street,
1890. Number of properties owned

While it is not possible to know the family circumstances and family structure of the Middle Park households, an analysis of the 1903 Electoral Roll for Middle Park (Southern Melbourne, Canterbury Ward) does hint at a relatively young, perhaps fairly recently married cohort. Almost all houses list only a married couple as the residents, and very rarely other household members old enough to be eligible to vote (then 21 years). While it was then not compulsory to enrol to vote, it would appear most eligible males and almost as many females did so. Perhaps the excitement of universal voting eligibility prompted such a response. So, given the rate of births in an age of no contraception (but, alas, high infant mortality), we can assume there were many young children in the suburb. Morris reports that by 1902 Middle Park School resorted to renting the Baptist Church on the corner of Kerferd Road and Richardson Street as an overflow space, and by 1910 numbers in the school had grown to over 1100.[13] Of course, it could also be the case that older offspring had married and left home, given the typically young marriage age. There were, however, some exceptions where several members of the same family at the same address were old enough to vote. For example The Buxton household, in addition to John and Mary, had Kathleen, Lorna and Mary (junior) all enrolled, as did the Ah Mouy family with Fon, King and Kum, and the Alston family's three children.

Changes during the last 100 years

By the eve of World War I, the majority of Middle Park sites had been developed, almost exclusively for housing. There were very few factories, and those there were generally 'clean' operations, such as Mardell's Hat Works, and Honeybone's hat block enterprise. As has been suggested, the population was initially slow to take up the advantages offered by the new suburb, and its growth was slowed by the economic depression of the first part of the 1890s. But once the effects of the depression ameliorated, faster development, and thus an increasing population was the pattern. As a new suburb, Middle Park seems to have attracted a wide variety of people of occupational and social status, thus it was perhaps always a 'middle-class' suburb which attracted few people of significant wealth, and probably excluded those of very low income. It was also perhaps an early example of a 'nation of homeowners' – though that status did not really about come until post-World War II. However, post-World War I the social composition of the suburb did change significantly, and saw it pass through perhaps three main subsequent phases; first to an area of multi- occupation of houses where larger houses were often divided into 'flats', and smaller homes took in boarders, with a consequent decline in social standing. Later, after World War II, it became home to many newly arrived, non-Anglo-Saxon migrants, especially Greek and Italian, but also a variety of others. And following that it moved through a phase of 'gentrification' where relatively wealthy, highly educated people moved in and 'rescued' many of the houses which were often showing signs of old age. By now Middle Park is about one hundred and fifty years old, and in many ways physically relatively unchanged, though the same cannot be said of the social composition of its residents.

Notes

[1]   Gresswell, D A, 1890, Report on the sanitary condition and sanitary administration of Melbourne and its suburbs, Vic Govt Printer.

[2]   Cannon, M, 1967, *The Land Boomers*, Melbourne University Press.

[3]   Priestley, S, 1995, *South Melbourne, a History*, Melbourne University Press.

[4]   See: e.g: Nankervis, M, 1998, Our Urban Parks; A suitable piece of real estate? *Journal .of Australian Studies*, V.22 (57), pp. 162–171.

[5]   Boyle, E, Montalto, Prabhupada House, in *Middle Park, from Swamp to Suburb*, Middle Park History Group, 2014, p. 61.

[6]   Priestley, S, 1995, *South Melbourne, a History*, Melbourne University Press.

[7]   Morris, G, 1987, No 2815. *Middle Park School, 1887–1987*, Middle Park Primary School. p. 11.

8   Note that house numbers changed frequently over the years as various subdivisions were effected. Many houses were without a number and went by house name. While there was an 'official' extensive council municipal wide re-numbering about 1903, re-numbering tended to continue until about World War I, by which time development of nearly all sites had occurred.

9   Cannon, M, 1967, *The Land Boomers*, Melbourne University Press.

10   See: Priestley, p. 240.

11   See: Priestley, p. 218.

12   See: Morris, p. 18.

Beaconsfield Parade, Middle Park, 2016

MIDDLE PARK: A BEACHSIDE SUBURB

Max Nankervis

Pre-history

The first recorded mention of the Middle Park beach was made in January-February 1803 when Charles Grimes and his crew in the *Cumberland*, all members of Captain Collins's settlement at Sorrento, which included the journal writer James Flemming, sailed up Port Phillip Bay on an exploratory tour of Port Phillip.[1] While the explorers do not appear to have actually traversed the land, the notes record various swamps around the Yarra River. But as they were visiting in January, the swamps were probably relatively dry.

But it was another three decades before any further European visits to the area. Those visits were made by John Batman and John Fawkner – both arriving across Bass Strait from the already established settlements in Tasmania. Before long there was European settlement in Sandridge (Port Melbourne) and St Kilda Hill. But the Middle Park area remained undeveloped, and a generally swampy area dominated by a line of sand dunes along the seafront edge, especially towards the northern section.

Early land use

However, while the area appears to have been formally unused, there are reports of some ad-hoc use, particularly by some 'Chinese fishermen' who established huts along the beach. Cooper, in his history of St Kilda notes the existence of Chinese huts on the West St Kilda Beach, the inhabitants of which were apparently moved-on or the huts demolished.[2] The 1859–60 Emerald Hill Rate Book noted a collection of eleven 'canvas and wood-framed huts' described as a 'Chinese village' which were valued at thirty-five pounds.

An 1864 map by Henry Cox, which includes the Middle Park beachfront area, appears to indicate some buildings in fenced enclosures along the foreshore, perhaps as part of a military installation, while an 1866 map by De Gruchy shows a (conjectured) residential subdivision.

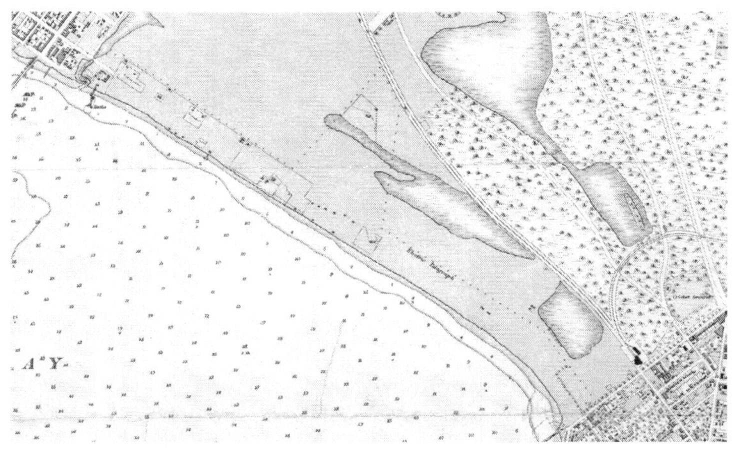

Cox map indicating some enclosures along the beach, 1864

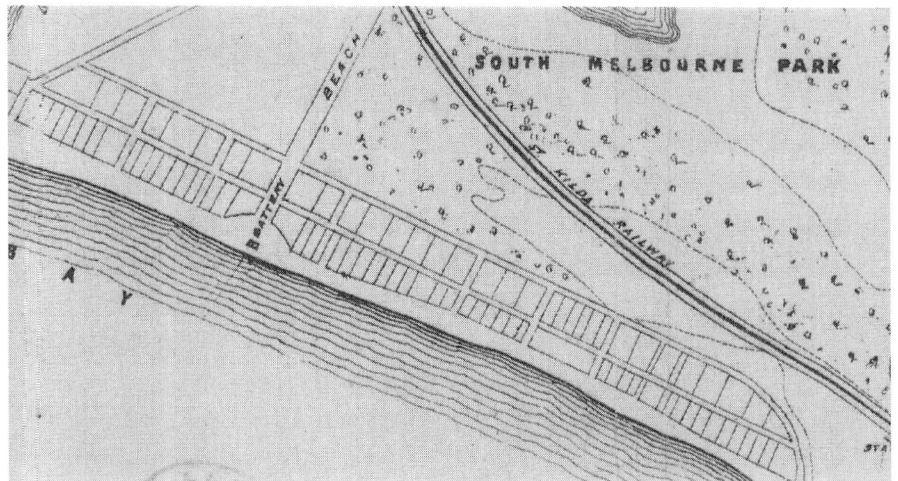

De Gruchy map showing conjectured roads and subdivision, 1866

Another use reported was for a Jewish retirement home in 1851,[3] auspiced by a Jamaican-born Jewish doctor, Dr Solomon Iffla.[4] This date is questionable as Dr Iffla may not have arrived in Melbourne before 1853,[5] and there is no record or image of the building.

But one use of the area which is better documented is the establishment of both fortification bases and an associated shooting range, 'The Butts', part of the Victorian colony's 'defence system'. One gun emplacement was located at the end of Kerferd Road, and the rifle range somewhere about where the Middle Park school yard is located today, although an early pupil at the school suggests differently and notes the backboard dune was still visible towards the beach from the school yard when he attended the school.[6]

From 1870 on there was obviously pressure on the Colonial government to release the Middle Park section for suburban development – an idea swept along by the spectacular property boom sweeping Melbourne. Today, residential development along a seafront – or indeed anywhere with a view of the sea – is seen as highly desirable and has an economic value to reflect this. But in the 19th century this feature was not given quite the same kudos. So the seafront value of Middle Park was not necessarily seen as its key advantage in the early years of development, and indeed the seafront sites were among the last sections to be fully developed.[7]

Despite its general neglect, it does appear that the potential of the seafront area for residential development was stirring some entrepreneurial minds as early as the 1860s with conjectured subdivisions shown on some maps. While the maps differ on the details, in general the proposals indicate two parallel roads, one along the beach and one immediately inland generally aligning with Beaconsfield Parade and Danks/Patterson/Park Streets, with intersecting cross streets at intervals. During the 1870s the surveying and subdivision did indeed produce a similar pattern of roads and sites.

Social and recreational activity

But while the sea was not a key attraction for most people, for a few hardy souls it did hold some attraction as a place of exercise and healthy recreation. Some reports suggest that even as early as 1840, some locals promenaded along the beach at Port Melbourne around Liardet's hotel in a sort of 'passeggiata'.[8] The only problem was that social morality and mores put significant restrictions on the use of the beach, especially the hours people were permitted to bathe. In general, bathing was prohibited. Nevertheless, from the earliest days of the colony, especially at nearby St Kilda, sea baths had been set up to cater for some of these hardy souls, including the even fewer hardy women.

But even in these enclosed and semi-private places swimwear was generally designed to cover much of the body, especially for ladies. In fact, rather than swimwear – for swimming was largely an unknown activity and seen as un-feminine – it was 'water-wear'. Any such water use costume was invariably made of heavy fabric – flannel or wool, and was almost a recipe for drowning should they be swept out to deeper water, unless the wearer was particularly fit.

But there are always social rebels, and it seems Middle Park had its few at least. For it appears that some bold men were said to be using the actual beach (and not the baths) for daylight swimming, exposed to the world for all to see. And part of the problem was that they were exposed for all to see fully. Unlike women, men rarely wore any swimming costume at all in the 19th century because, for the most part, it was an activity shared only by (a few) men in a location in which few self-respecting women would be found. This problem of 'exposure' was the basis of complaints at Kenny's baths in St Kilda as early as the 1850s. But amidst the community horror the Council felt constrained to act, and so in a compromise, it allowed swimming on the beach in the early morning and evening. Despite this some rebels continued their revolt and swam during the day. But by the end of the century, swimming costumes for both men and women came into general use, though they nevertheless continued the cover-up in the famous neck-to-knee costumes, made of perhaps lighter fabrics than flannel, but still not designed for smooth flow through the water. And for the growing numbers using Middle Park beach, it would have been the normal attire.

Blake family in swimming costumes, about 1919

There was, however, one other avenue for male swimmers which to an extent settled the problem of social mores. For a while it appears some baths held men-only sessions and some baths were exclusively for men where men swam and sunbathed in the nude, and it seems the practice continued until complaints about the men being (partially) visible from the beach through the lattice-work surrounding fence brought in regulations in the 1940s to prohibit this. However the practice continued at least until 1954 when the daily paper, the *Argus*, proclaimed; 'Women to invade male swimmers nude refuge'.[9] It seems a beach inspector invaded for the first time in 30 years the 'sacred nude bathing place for men' and bluntly told the men: 'Put some clothes on': The startled males, accustomed for years to the freedom of nudity in their regular swims obeyed – wearing a towel to the water's edge, then swimming in the nude. But it didn't go down easily. One Victorian M.P., a regular visitor, soon started a rebellion against the order. 'Be blowed to it. Some of us have been swimming here in the nude since we were boys', he announced and was supported by other local men – including some notable and powerful Melbourne businessmen who frequently used the pool. But their days of nude swimming were over. While the Town Clerk, Mr Cox, denied any knowledge of an order for the raid it had already been decided that the baths were to revert to mixed bathing in the new year, Council having already amended a by-law to permit mixed bathing, though the change had yet to be approved by the Governor in Council.

But eventually the local South Melbourne Council was forced to fall into line with social movements and regulations in that northern city of sin, Sydney. For in 1904, William Gocher, who frequently swam at Manly beach and was owner of the *Manly and North Sydney News*, a leading figure in the Manly Progress Association, and a failed candidate for all three levels of politics (as well as being strongly anti-Semitic), wore a short, revealing (by the standards of the day) swimsuit and swam during the day. Various attempts by beach inspectors to fine him just enhanced and widened the revolt, and so Council gave-in. Other jurisdictions soon followed – at least for men.

But for women the older-style apparel continued probably until after World War I. However there was nevertheless a worldwide female swimwear revolution led by an Australian female swimmer, Annette Kellerman, who designed a tight, body hugging (and shape-revealing) swimsuit which gradually gained wider acceptance.[10]

Post-war beach

Just when this fashion of more revealing bathers hit Middle Park beach is unknown, but certainly by the 1930s more and more flesh was exposed on the beach as extant photos reveal. Nevertheless, a 1920s photo of Middle Park beach indicates that many women still saw the place as a fully clothed relaxation spot, in contrast to men. Women, more commonly only used the beach as a sitting place, sitting fully clothed while perhaps supervising children playing in the sand as the photo suggests.

Mrs May Clements with daughter and granddaughter
on Middle Park beach early 1930s

World War I brought many social (and economic) changes, and among those changes was the use of the seafront and beaches, especially as a recreation facility. While that war was not necessarily as liberating for women as was World War II, it did introduce a less socially constricted world. Some of this liberation came in the form of beach wear and the protocols of beach use. No longer was the beach the province of unclad men, thus keeping respectable ladies well clear of the water. Beach dress codes were finally relaxed to allow more suitable attire (for both sexes) – though neck-to knee was still common. But for the bolder beach-goers, especially the young, relatively short bathers were acceptable, though for men a 'skirt-front' was often regulated, while women still made some pretence at wearing a sort of dress as part of their costume.

Cameron family and friends on Middle Park beach, 1944

But what was noticeable was the more frequent use of the beach by the broader population. Not surprisingly then Middle Park beachfront became a popular destination, not only of locals, but for the residents of hinterland suburbs. Along with the mad excitement of the 1920s with its flappers Charleston-ing around the dance floor and sometime with cigarettes in hand, the 1930s emerged as an era of a much more 'outdoors' lifestyle for the whole family. Not only could adults plunge in and swim (though as many could not swim, swimming lessons were becoming popular), but the children could bring buckets and spades to build castles.

A rare photograph of Middle Park beach opposite the Good Shepherd Convent laundry complex shows the density of beach usage on a good day.

Middle Park beach in the 1920s with the Good Shepherd Convent complex in the background

World War II brought about even greater social changes – with concomitant loosening of restrictions on all sorts of behaviour. And while nearby St Kilda had become something of a social cesspool during and after the war, as artists like John Perceval and Danila Vassilieff expressed and exposed in their art, some of that looseness spilled over to more genteel and respectable Middle Park. And some of that behaviour would have been evident on the beachfront as some newspaper reports suggest that there were 'undesirables' lurking. Just how problematic was this influx is unclear, but probably little different from any inner urban area of the time, and perhaps better than its northern and southern neighbours. In the 1950 and 1960s Middle Park became home to European migrants from many countries, though especially Greece – people who on the whole were interested in being accepted and in making a future, not trouble. But based on time constraints alone, they were less likely to use the beach for recreation – except for that international pastime, fishing.

But from the 1970s on there was another social shift which had some effect on the beach use. Middle Park was one of the first inner urban areas to 'gentrify' as CURA data suggests.[11] This brought about an influx of relatively higher-educated, young people who did put a high value on outdoor and sporting activities, which included swimming and sailing – though less on fishing. But even so, Middle Park beach was generally a deserted stretch on most days, and only gradually over the next two decades did the crowds once more begin to flock to the beach, a flow which was both the cause of and a result of beachside improvements and new infrastructure. Along with this came an influx of even more daring beachwear all designed to display an all-Australian tan, a process which later came to be strongly discouraged by the 'slip, slop, slap' government sponsored program based on the proven relationship of suntan (or burn) with skin cancer. Nevertheless, the fashion of brief men's bathers and topless swimwear for women was certainly a feature of life on the beach in the 1970s, as the famed social photographer, the late Rennie Ellis, demonstrated so clearly in the pictorial essay, *Life's a Beach*.

Four buskers at Middle Park Beach 1985

Getting there

From the earliest days there had been a road off St Kilda Road leading towards the coast. Originally called Three Chain Road, or Beach Road – a road complete with a toll booth near St Kilda Road – it was originally essentially for access to the military installations. It was later re-named Albert Road, and its extension past the railway line, Kerferd Road. But until the 1870s there appears to have been no official direct access to the Middle Park beach section, though it is likely that the area had various tracks which, in the summer at least, as the lagoons or swamps dried up, were passable.

But by the early 20th century as beach usage became more fashionable (and less restricted), better access was called for. To assist people getting to the beach, as well as commuting transport for the increasing population of Middle Park, the electric tram line to St Kilda beach was newly laid and opened in 1926. It trundled along Danks/Patterson/Park Streets just a block back from the beachfront giving excellent access to the beach. In addition, the train line, now, electrified, made the journey, at least from the city, easy, and faster. Thus, for most of the then population of suburban Melbourne, the beach was less than an hour's ride away.

Despite car ownership being just in its infancy, it was possible to drive to the beach, and Beaconsfield Parade provided ample parking for those lucky, or rich enough to own a car. Photographs of the period indicate a smattering of cars along the beach road. And for the locals it was a short walk, though decorum seemed to demand that one should leave the beach suitably attired in street clothes. One long-time resident relates how she and her sister were photographed by a daily newspaper journalist bedecked in bathers returning from the beach. While it seems not everyone approved of such boldness, it does indicate how 'times they were a-changin'.

Beachside residential development

As has been suggested, access to the beach was not seen to be a prime desirable residential feature in the 19th century. While it had an attraction for some as a place for active recreation such as swimming, for most part it was a place visited and where one looked on from a discreet distance when the elements were not too challenging.

For this reason, Beaconsfield Parade was slower to develop in comparison with the rest of Middle Park. More attractive were the main traffic streets where one's affluence could be well-displayed and Canterbury Road better served this purpose and was more densely developed at an earlier date. The chart below, a comparison of the site development of Canterbury Road and Beaconsfield Parade shows this lag, and highlights the period at which the beach did start to become a desirable residential location – around the time of World War I, and especially after. While Canterbury Road was about three quarters developed by 1895, the same proportion of Beaconsfield Parade sites developed did not occur until about 1920, a period when outdoor activity became more fashionable and Middle Park beach became more popular as a recreation destination.

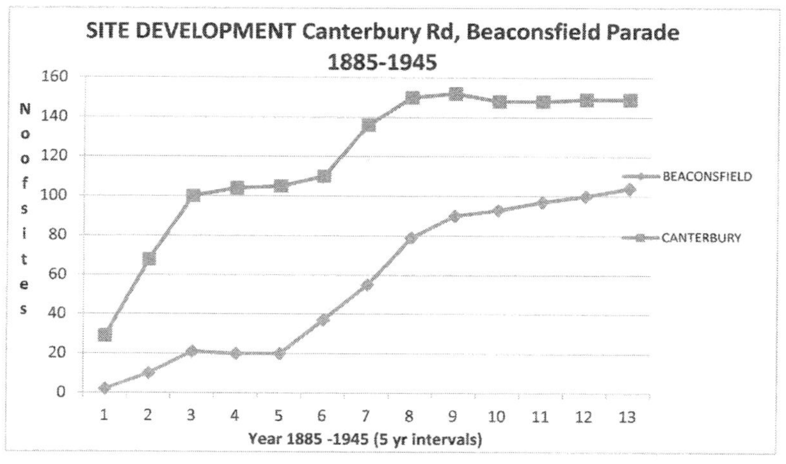

Rate of site development Beaconsfield Parade and Canterbury Road compared, 1885–1945. (Data based on Sands & McDougall Directories)

But Beaconsfield Parade was not all residential development. Perhaps the most dominating development along the road was the Good Shepherd Convent, a facility run by the Good Shepherd sisters from about 1892 up to the 1970s at which time the land was sold for various redevelopments, including some public housing of (for its time) innovative design. Its dominance can be seen in the photograph on page 98.

Beach facilities

But as well as the beach being more accessible, it was made more attractive with various facilities – changing rooms, 'kiosks' and even shaded seating structures.

Of particular heritage interest are the small covered shelters spread along the beach which were built around 1914. Only one of these shaded structures is extant in the Middle Park stretch today and another can be found in Albert Park, although old photos suggest there were several more along the beachfront. But both the general ravages of the weather and storms, and also, alas, vandalism, have forced constant maintenance. Indeed the remaining unit has even been set alight by vandals, and so it is something like the 'woodsman's axe' – still original, but has had six new handles and four new blades.

Of course, there have always been facilities for buying drinks and other refreshments. Most of the very early refreshment outlets have long gone and been replaced by more modern buildings, and today there is only one left along the Middle Park stretch, that at the Harold Alexander Pavilion having only recently been demolished. This small outlet not only dispensed icecreams, sweets and coffee, but provided a handy rental income for the Life Saving Club. The proprietor, Mr David O'Dwyer tells the story of how in the 1980s he also procured a boat cheaply and added to the income by dragging the boat along the beach loaded with watermelon which he sold in slices to thirsty beachgoers.[12]

Beach shelters on Middle Park beach, c. 1920

Perhaps the most practical facility was changing rooms. Several of these facilities were located along the beachfront. Aerial photos, such as those on pages 98 and 120, show the facility at Mills and McGregor Streets, though there were changing room structures at most other intersecting streets. The Mills Street structure remains, though on a more reduced scale. And, in line with today's social patterns, the building is primarily now a licensed kiosk/restaurant with a terrace literally on the beach.

Also catering for swimmers were several swimming and diving platforms, anchored about 100 metres off-shore. Two of these can be seen in the water either side of Middle Park baths in aerial photomaps of 1931 up to the 1950s. They are highlighted in the picture below, an aerial photo from about 1951.

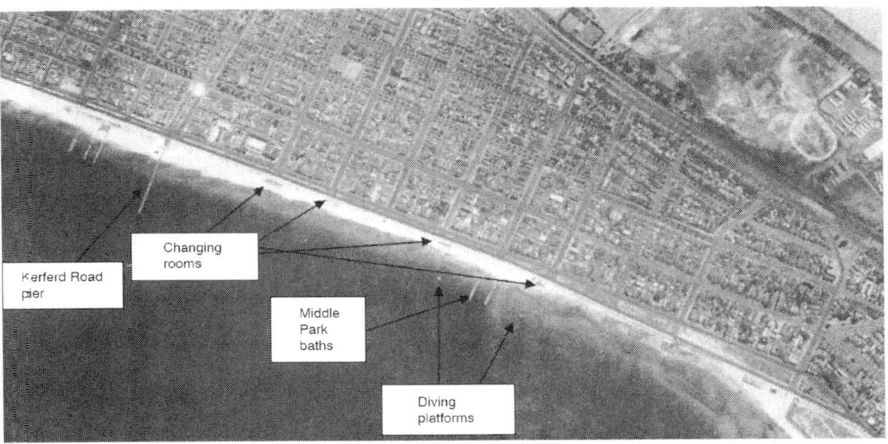

Above: Overhead photo map of Middle Park beach, 1951, indicating various facilities

Left: Diving platform off the beach near Middle Park Baths

Sea baths

But perhaps the most visually dominant structure was the Middle Park Baths dating from the 1890s which was just one of several such structures around the bay, the earliest being Captain Kenny's baths located in an old ship hulk just near the St Kilda pier. There were also 'ladies baths' just north of Kerferd Road in Albert Park. The Middle Park Baths, designed by local architect, Thomas Ashworth, were built about 1891, and sat projecting out of the water at the end of Armstrong Street. Old photographs show just how dominant this structure was as part of the urban landscape, while aerial photographs/maps show how far they extended out to sea.

Middle Park Baths, c. 1910

The concept of sea baths derives from that Victorian preoccupation with shielding prying eyes from those bold enough to take the waters. Though they also originally had a more practical use in an era where bathrooms were not necessarily a part of homes. They were quite literally 'baths' (e.g. Melbourne City Baths). However, probably all houses in Middle Park were built in an age when bathrooms were an integral part of household facilities, and so the Middle Park baths were probably always much more of a recreational facility. Nevertheless, the baths were still in use up to the 1950s, providing the opportunity for males to still swim in the nude until about 1954 when this scandalous behaviour was the subject of heated Council debate.

However, like much 19th century infrastructure that began life in private, commercial ownership, when profits fell it was not unusual for governments of various levels to pick up the unprofitable remains and incur the losses as an important 'public good'. And this, it seems, is the story and fate of the baths which began as a private company, the Middle Park Sea Bathing Company. At a Council meeting in February 1912, Council voted to buy out the sea baths company for two hundred pounds, having upped their original offer of one hundred pounds when the company secretary pointed out that they had been offered almost a higher amount just as scrap.[13] A similar story befell the seabaths at St Kilda in 1918.[14]

But popular as they were, the baths had had their moments; not only from the ravages of the elements, but as a financial burden, as Council reports indicate. In the end it was the collision of storm damage, and finance which combined to bring about their demise. In 1951 a severe storm carried away significant parts of the structure as had occurred before on several occasions, and a further damaging storm in 1960 was such that the cost of repairs could not be justified, especially since at that time the usage levels had significantly declined.[15] A decision was made to demolish the baths. And so the wonderful visual punctuation at the end of Armstrong Street at Beaconsfield Parade became a blank sheet.

View along Armstrong Street with baths building as a terminal view point

Another important piece of infrastructure was the Kerferd Road pier. While technically in Albert Park, along with the adjoining Albert Park Yachting and Angling Club, it can be considered as part of the Middle Park beach infrastructure. The current pier structure was apparently built in two stages, the first 360 feet in 1887 and an additional 300 feet in 1889; although it is believed there was some form of pier in this location since at least 1881.[16] But piers, including Kerferd Road pier, were important promenading routes, a place to see and be seen as people began to accept the beach as a recreational venue, albeit, initially for most, a fully clothed venue.

Though, as with other beach infrastructure, the pier suffered from the ravages of weather and vandalism and occasionally there were suggestions of total demolition which fortunately have come to nothing.

Alongside the Kerferd Road pier is the Albert Park Yachting and Angling Club which occupies a Heritage-listed building, dating from around 1909, though over the years has undergone various modernisations and refurbishments which have altered its original appearance.[17] Today the club has become more of a social club, though it does have its collection of members interested in fishing and some fishing boats are still stored in its basement, but the wooden gantry used to bring these to the water appears to be no longer in use. While the club did engage in sailing regattas in its early days this activity does seem to have waned in its appeal to members. In earlier days, the fishing boats were often equipped with sails enabling longer and more distant fishing expeditions, though for the most part fishermen rowed their boats out into the bay.

While there is a local yacht club at Port Melbourne and another at St Kilda (The Royal Melbourne Yacht Squadron – originally St Kilda Yacht Club), there appears to have been some pressure to create a sail haven for boats in the area, especially around the Kerferd Road pier and the Yachting and Angling Club. As early as 1887 a correspondent to the *Argus* was suggesting the need for a safe breakwater at St Kilda to protect the yachts of the St Kilda Sailing (yacht) Club.[18] And in 1910 Minister Baillieu, along with several other ministers and public servants, including Mr Catani, walked along the beach from Port Melbourne to Sandringham to investigate the need for safer yachting facilities.[19] This may have been partly prompted by a request to develop Kerferd Road pier with some form of breakwater to help sailors. But apparently Mr Baillieu felt the concept was 'too pretentious' and suggested he would only financially assist something simpler.

A rather more unusual beach related infrastructure was the (apparently) open-air 'Beach Theatre' at no. 107 (now 108–110) Beaconsfield Parade (the street numbers change). While this venue was clearly in Albert Park rather than Middle Park, it does offer an insight into the 'festive' nature of the beachfront. Mrs Emily McLaren is listed as operating a 'Beach Theatre' from about 1913 to 1923, although it is sometimes referred to as 'St Louis Theatre' and later the 'Strand Theatre'. Meanwhile just along the street at the Victoria Hotel at Kerferd Road at 'The Vic' – another (indoor) picture theatre operated for some years. Sometime in the 1990s the St Louis/Strand site was redeveloped as a block of modern units, though under pressure from South Melbourne Council's Heritage Planners, the facade of the theatre site was retained and is still there today with the name St Louis across the doorway arch which, it is assumed, was the entrance to the theatre.

More festive infrastructure was nearby on the beach where a carnival type set-up was located and the beach wall was rebuilt to accommodate this. The carousel from this site was apparently moved to Canberra's Civic area.

The seawall

One of the most dominant structures along the beach is the bluestone wall which extends from Station pier to St Kilda pier. It is unclear when the earliest protection of the beach road was constructed, but a Henry Gritten painting of Sandridge (Port Melbourne) in 1866 with the London Hotel in the background shows a wooden palisade fence apparently delineating the beach from the hinterland, presumably to stop sand drifts. Whether any such simple barrier existed in the Middle Park section is unclear, but St Kilda Council's records show that in 1865 the lower esplanade was repeatedly being washed away by storms and the Council, assisted by the Colonial Government, constructed a 'sea wall of stone pitchers'.

*Section of an 1866 painting by Henry Gritten showing a
simple fence delineating the beach from the hinterland.*

But Council (and those pressing for its construction) clearly felt that the job of financing the wall should not fall solely on Council, and frequent calls for State (or Colonial) assistance were made and forthcoming. After all, the argument went, the beach was a 'public good' enjoyed by a wider audience than just the local residents.

Other records suggest that a wall was begun to be constructed as late as 1898 and was completed about 1927. A report to Council indicates that, at least in one section, there was a 'light ornamental retaining wall designed to give a finish at footpath line and prevent sand blowing onto the street'.[20] The more substantial (presumably bluestone) wall was constructed in 1898, though it seems it lacked a concrete 'toe' and suffered erosion from high tides. But even after the 'toe' was constructed tides and extreme weather still continued the eroding process. After 1925 groynes were constructed to ameliorate the erosion, and can be seen in photographs. However these groynes were destroyed by wave action as the actual waterline moved closer to the wall. For example, in the 1970s at almost any Spring (high) tide the waves were right up to the seawall and various rocks were exposed. The erosion also severely undermined the Harold Alexander Pavilion opposite Armstrong Street which had to be demolished.

But the seawall continued to be a financial thorn in Council's side. And so, for example, in April 1908, a group of councillors, in tandem with the members of the Albert Park Bowling Club (who were likely to have been the same men), invited the Premier Mr (later Sir) Thomas Bent to afternoon tea at the club, apparently with the intention of luring him down to the seashore to observe the erosion issues with the seawall.[21] On this occasion he offered to put it to Cabinet that the State Government allocate 1000 pounds on the basis that Council contribute the 2000 pounds balance. Given the efforts put into 'duchessing' Mr Bent by cheering for his health, and massaging his considerable ego, it is likely the grant was forthcoming.

Storms washing over the seawall, c. 1920s

But the problem persisted in part, claimed some, because the solutions tried were only 'band aid'. Even in 2005, Councillor Ray complained that the beach was especially vulnerable because a breakwater in St Kilda harbour, built to shelter boats during the 1956 Olympic Games, blocked sand from drifting to Middle Park beach. The Councillor also argued that previous solutions, such as dumping 30,000 cubic metres of sand on the Middle Park–West St Kilda section after a severe storm in December 1999, was only ever a temporary measure. A more permanent solution such as building rock groynes was necessary. Against this, a coastal geomorphologist, Mr Eric Bird, said rock groynes would not have prevented the sand being washed away because they only prevent sand moving *along* the coast and would not prevent the waves combing the sand from the beach to the sea floor. Despite the ravages of the weather necessitating rebuilding of sections at various times, the wall remains and for the most part prevents waves from spilling onto the road and excess sand drifts.

Landscaping

Probably as part of the late 19th century work to control erosion, Beaconsfield Parade, including the median strip, was landscaped, generally in the late Victorian garden style of rockwork and shrubs. Early photographs of the road show something of the style of this planting and landscaping.

An early photograph of the Beaconsfield Parade showing the planting in the median strip.

In 1901 Mr Albert Aughtie became City Engineer and in 1927 went on a study tour during which he took a particular interest in beach erosion structures and landscaping On his return he appears to have put considerable energy into redeveloping the Albert Park and Middle Park beachfront by resetting the sea wall, laying out lawns and building concrete paths, as well as renovating the Middle Park Baths. It was perhaps at this time that the Victorian landscaping was replaced with the simpler style of lawns, concrete kerbing and less planting, more or less as we see it today. It is probably the Aughtie improvements which remained until a significant redesign of the seafront in the 1980s. But by that time the ravages of the wind and salt air had killed all but the hardiest vegetation and the footpath pavers were uneven and dangerous. Several forces converged to bring about a change.

Firstly there were the newer 'gentrifiers' who used the beach much more, and were more demanding in their calls for improvements to inner urban infrastructure of all sorts. But it was also an era in town planning concepts where 'urban design' was taking over from a more utilitarian approach. Infrastructure (and buildings), it was argued, should not only be useful but should look good. The catalyst idea for the palm planting came from a local nurseryman, Peter McGain, who had seen a similar scheme on a visit to Santa Barbara in California. Through a combined council landscape committee (St Kilda, South Melbourne and Port Melbourne) they approached the state government for funding. This drive for urban aesthetics was fortunate in having both a Planning Minister, Evan Walker, and a Head of the Planning Department, David Yencken, both architects, and funding was forthcoming. The result was one of the most dramatic visual changes to the area. Over several years, large, hardy and generally successfully transplanted Canary Island Palm Trees were purchased and transported from various sites and private gardens around Melbourne and replanted along the beachside of Beaconsfield Parade. Along with this a separate bike path to cater for the growing number of recreational and commuter cyclists was laid out parallel to the pedestrian path. Later, somewhat less mature palms were planted on the inland side of the road, and some tall Washington Palms were also planted in the median strip at the intersection of the 'cross streets'. The result was something of a visual coup, transforming the bleak stretch of road into something resembling a Mediterranean or Southern Californian beach resort.

Storm damage

While for the most part, Port Phillip Bay is a reasonably benign stretch of water, on occasions it can throw up severe storms and damaging waves. Even as early as 1836, and 1849 some of the more dramatic storms were reported in the daily press. One particular storm which came with intense fury and speed occurred in 1918 and a report describes the impact and how roofing iron was blown about the beach, fortunately not severely injuring fleeing beachgoers as they hurried off the beach. But alas, for many they fled without their street clothes which were whipped away in the maelstrom and lost. Fortunately it seems other generous locals came to their rescue and provided blankets and clothing.[22] In another devastating storm in 1949 the Middle Park Baths apparently sustained considerable damage with nearly 20 feet of the outer end of the baths washed away and 12 dressing sheds were demolished. Despite the ferocity, the baths manager, Mr H. Thomas, and his brother-in-law swam around saving fittings.[23] A further storm in 1951 raised the issue of the cost of repairing the baths.[24] Finally following a storm in 1960 the baths were closed and demolished.

But even without storms, the natural flow of the tides washes up various weed and detritus, and so the beach requires cleaning. The photographs below show the contrast in the equipment used to do the job in the 1950s and today.

Beach cleaning, c. 1950s and in 2016

Swimming activities and life saving

While, despite the restrictions, in the 19th century some brave souls did use the beach for swimming, the knowledge or ability to swim was not widespread, and thus the sea remained a slightly dangerous place for many. Nevertheless, even from the earliest days there were swimming carnivals and races which attracted a spectator audience. Captain Kenny apparently held swimming races at his baths in the 1840s and charged spectators to enter to watch.[25] And early in the 20th century there are numerous press reports of swimming races and meetings involving Middle Park locals. A swimming club was in evidence in Middle Park by at least 1910 and was engaged in National Championships.

But some people did recognise the importance of being able to swim. While it is likely that many local youths were reasonably adept at swimming simply by dint of living by the sea, Middle Park Primary School headmaster, Henry Tisdall, even in 1894, was ensuring pupils could swim by enabling swimming lessons at the local baths.[26]

Swimming Carnivals were held at the Middle Park Baths, though unlike the luxury of our filtered and generally enclosed pools today, the swimmers had to often deal with the elements. At one carnival in February 1914, the winning swimmer was just about to touch the end of the final lap when he was dashed against the planks and sustained facial damage.[27]

Middle Park girls swimming team about 1921

But by the 1930s swimming, both as a recreational and serious sport, was well-entrenched in the sporting calendar. By then even women were taking part in swimming races. One report in 1910 – along with a discussion of the vexed issue of 'mixed bathing', reports on a women's swimming competition at Stubbs (ladies) Baths (in Albert Park) where Miss Fanny Durak, who at the age of 14 years came third against Annette Kellerman, the lady internationally famous (or notorious) for her revealing swimming costume.[28]

As well as swimming, water polo was another beach-based sport, water polo teams were associated with the clubs, including the Middle Park club.

View of Middle Park beach from baths towards McGregor Street showing changing rooms, and a mystery structure. It may have been a navigation facility.

Excitement

But while storms and waves gave some excitement to beach-goers, and even some amusement, other events were a little more concerning. One episode concerned a couple of 19 year old lads from Middle Park, one from a particularly well-known family, the Honeybones, along with his mate, F. Whitehead. It seems that early on the morning of 23 December, 1898, just days before Christmas they were out fishing for flathead about a half mile offshore. Suddenly they felt a heavy bump under their boat and looked over to see a shark, approximately 12 foot long with its teeth into the boat. They beat it off with an oar, but it returned again to seize the front of the boat and then, after beating it off again, it returned for a third attack. However it finally retreated and they rowed back to shore where they inspected the damage – observing clear teeth marks in the hull. Another (or the same) shark was reported nearby the previous day.[29]

One of the more amusing episodes occurred in 1935 when two workers working off Middle Park on an improvised pontoon made of planks strapped to fuel cans were in the process of repairing a diving tower damaged in a storm the previous December. A strong northerly wind blew-up and sent the pontoon 600 metres out to sea with Henry Wallace, a local Middle Park lad, and another man from Hawthorn, clinging to the pontoon. Fortunately another workman on the beach at the St Kilda Yacht Club (now Royal Melbourne Yacht Squadron) came to the rescue of the men in the club boat just as they were lashing themselves to the pontoon to avoid being washed off.[30]

But the beach has also been the site of tragedy and even murder. Just as tragic was the apparent murder-suicide of a couple on Middle Park beach on 17 November 1896. An enquiry found that the situation arose because Mrs Quinn told Mr Watson that her real husband was alive, thus they were not (or could not be) sure they were legally husband and wife. Indeed two marriage certificates were found near the bodies. In such a sad and desperate situation they felt constrained to end their lives and went to Middle Park beach (presumably with a weapon) with the intention of doing this together. But while Mr Watson fatally shot Mrs Quinn, and then himself in the head, he only managed to critically injure himself and survived, even though following the shooting he tried to drown himself. Subsequently he was charged with murder, found guilty and given the death sentence, but the jury noted that as the couple had intended to both die, and recognising their situation, they strongly appealed for mercy.[31]

Today

Today the beach is seen as a key attraction of Middle Park. Locals and others alike come to use the beach in various ways. For some it is to swim, for others simply to lie in the sun with an occasional foray into the water. But for others it is for more active water sports like wind or kite surfing, while for others it is merely to sit on or beside the beach for a social chat and a coffee. Just as the Albert Park clearly defines Middle Park on its northern side, the beach defines its boundary on the southern side. Middle Park is very much defined by its proximity to the beach.

Notes

[1] Flemming, James, A Journal of Grimes' Survey. The Cumberland in Port Phillip, January–February 1803.

[2] Rate Books, Emerald Hill, 1856. See also: Cooper, p. 103, & 238. (Note: Heritage Victoria notes seven huts).

[3] Daley, C, 1940, *The history of South Melbourne: from the foundation of settlement at Port Phillip to the year 1938*, by order for the Council of the City of South Melbourne, p. 36.

[4] Priestley, S, 1995, *South Melbourne: A History*, MUP, p. 79.

[5] Grogan, R, 2007, *Commodores, Colonials and Councillors*, Cygnet, Melbourne, p. 39.

[6] Morris, G, *Middle Park School, 1887–1987*, Middle Park Primary School, p. 5.

[7] *Middle Park; from Swamp to suburb*, MPHG, 2014, p. 85ff.

[8] Barnard, J, 2008, *Jetties and piers: a background history of maritime infrastructure in Victoria*, Heritage Victoria.

9   The *Argus*, 22 December 1954, p. 1.

10   The *Register*, Thursday, 11 July 1912, p. 6.

11   Centre for Urban Research and Action, 1977, *The displaced: a study of housing conflict Melbourne inner city*, p. 11.

12   Personal communication. David O'Dwyer.

13   The *Argus*, Thursday, 8 February 1912.

14   Cooper, J, 1931, *A History of St Kilda 1840–1931*, p. 180.

15   South Melbourne Council minutes, 1960.

16   Heritage Victoria; H1534, Kerferd Road pier.

17   See http://www.apyac.org.au/about/history/

18   Neale, R, 1984, *Jolly dogs are we*, Landscape Publications.

19   *Argus*, Friday, 1 July 1910, p. 8.

20   *Argus*, Friday, 29 July 1927.

21   *Argus*, 21 April 1908, p. 7.

22   *Melbourne Leader*, 9 February 1918, p. 26.

23   *Argus*, Monday, 17 January 1949, p. 3.

24   *Record*, Saturday, 5 May 1951, p. 7.

25   See Cooper, ibid., p. 164.

26   Morris, ibid., p. 26.

27   *Argus*, Monday, 2 February 1914.

28   *Express and Telegraph*, 25 February 1910, p. 3.

29   *Argus*, 9 February 1918, p. 26.

30   The *Mercury*, Tuesday, 19 March 1935, p. 10.

31   *Sydney Morning Herald*, 1897.

THE MIDDLE PARK BOWLING CLUB

David South

Early history

The game of lawn bowls, as it is played today, was developed in Scotland in the second half of the 19th century; though there is evidence that people have been playing games that involve rolling a ball towards some fixed point for thousands of years. Lawn bowls was introduced into Australia by Scottish immigrants in the 1860s, and bowling clubs were set up in the inner suburbs of Melbourne from this time. By 1900, there were thirty-three bowling clubs in Melbourne.

In this area of Melbourne while there had been some settlements along Canterbury Road, and along what later became Beaconsfield Parade, Middle Park as a suburb was in its infancy in 1900. Despite this, and despite the fact that there were seven bowling clubs fairly close by (two of them were actually in the Albert Park Reserve, one on Fitzroy Street in St Kilda, and another attached to the South Melbourne Cricket Club at their oval), it was nevertheless thought important for Middle Park to have its own bowling club.

A preliminary meeting was held at the Middle Park Hotel (then known as Mahon's Hotel) on 20 June 1903, to consider the securing of a portion of the Reserve in Middle Park for the purpose of bowling, lawn tennis, quoits etc. A deputation was appointed to wait on the trustees. The ground having been secured, the Middle Park Bowling and Recreation Club was formed on 23 September 1903, at a meeting in Honeybone's Hall. Despite its name, it was a bowling club.

The greens

The first priority was to construct a bowling green. This was done by Mr G. W. Horsfall, curator of the Royal Melbourne Golf Club course which at this time was in Sandringham. The bowling green was built during 1905, and was originally 165 ft by 156 ft. In 1911 the North-South dimension was reduced from 156 ft to 120 ft, in compliance with a decision to standardise green size throughout Australia. In 1975 the green was widened to 56 metres (183 ft).

Middle Park bowling green

Lights were installed on the green in 1914, and replaced by new lights in 1961. These were removed in 1975, apparently as an indirect consequence of the adoption of Daylight Saving Time in 1971. It was now light enough to play bowls until quite late in summer, and the increasingly elderly members were not willing to come out at night.

In January 2012 the green was converted from Kentucky Bent Grass (a winter grass) to Tifdwarf (a summer grass). This enables use through the winter. It is understood Bent grasses were introduced in Victoria after the war, as a better surface than the common couch then in use.

In 1910 a second green was constructed at the rear of the Club buildings. It had been expanded to its current size by 1918. Lights were installed in 2005, and the green was converted from Bent grass to Tifdwarf in January 2010.

In 1971 an additional three rink green was constructed on the northern boundary of the club. This was converted to a summer grass over Christmas 2004.

The Club has had a reputation for top class greens since 1924, and this is clearly due to the expertise of the greenkeepers. One reason is that greenkeepers stayed for quite long periods – R. W. Hoskin from 1924 to 1936, Alan Vance from 1940 to 1971, Maurie Mayes from 1978 to 1992, and Adrian Marston from 1992 to the present time. The Bowls Associations regularly used the Middle Park Bowling Club greens for Pennant finals, and for other important games. The semi-finals and finals of games in the 12th Australian Bowling Carnival in 1946 were held on Middle Park's greens, and the pattern was repeated the next time the Australian Bowling Carnival was held in Victoria, in 1954.

Middle Park Bowling Club, 1962

The buildings

The original pavilion was erected during 1905, at a total cost of £166. This picture opposite was taken at the opening of the green in 1905. The money was raised by issuing debentures – essentially, borrowing from the members. This building was never demolished, but was added to, and was altered.

Middle Park Bowling Club opening, 1905

In 1914 there were major extensions to the Clubhouse, at a cost of £400, and in 1918 a Ladies Clubhouse was erected, and a Caretakers cottage, at a cost of £750.

This was what the main building and the Caretakers cottage looked like in 1921.

Club and caretakers cottage

In 1936 at the opening of the new pavilion it appeared as follows.

New pavilion for bowlers

And this was the original Ladies Clubhouse as it appeared in the opening of the 1928 season.

Original Ladies Clubhouse

These buildings gave the Middle Park Bowling Club some of the best facilities in Melbourne.

Brick veneer extension

There were continued internal renovations, but the next major building program was the addition of a brick veneer structure in 1955. The external appearance has not been substantially altered, so it looked then much as it looks today. It cost £13,000 to put up and fit out. Again, the money was raised by issuing debentures. The loans were not fully repaid until 1974.

In 1969 $1184 was spent on the construction of a ladies toilet and a Ladies Lounge in the main Club building, perhaps increasing acceptance of the role of women in the Club – though they still had their own clubhouse.

There were some major building works in the mid 1970s – in effect, when the loans for the 1955 extension to the building were finally paid out. The main club rooms were extended to include extensive locker rooms, the building was refurbished internally, and the whole building clad with an imitation brick surface, replacing the ageing weatherboards. This work was funded by a loan of $30,000 from the Albert Park Committee of Management, and loans from members.

Refurbished main club rooms with imitation brick cladding

The patio overlooking the back green was added, with ironwork railing made by a member who had a senior position in the Victorian Railways workshops, and the ironwork was put together there – presumably at Railways expense. This method of getting things done was not uncommon in clubs of all kinds.

Detail of wrought iron railing

In 1982 the Ladies Pavilion and the Greenkeepers cottage, constructed in 1918, were demolished, and replaced by a new building, which incorporated a three-bedroom residence for the greenkeeper and ladies clubrooms. This was funded by a loan from the bank. The cost of the work was $33,000. It was built by volunteer members.

In 1983 the 'dome' shown in early photographs was removed, and replaced by a new roof. In 1985 $21,000 was spent on a refurbishment of the main clubrooms. A suspended ceiling was installed over the dance floor, and a second evaporative cooler installed over the dance floor. This was replaced in 2012. The building works from 1970 to 1985 were largely at the instigation of member Kevin Mayes, who was a builder. His brother Maurie was the greenkeeper from 1978 to 1992.

New Ladies Pavilion

In the mid 1990s, Melbourne Parks and Waterways, the landlords, insisted that no-one live within the park, and the Greenkeeper's cottage was vacated. In 1995 when the Grand Prix track was constructed, the Victorian Race Walkers Club took over the unit to use as a clubhouse – an arrangement that continues to the present day. By Act of Parliament the Grand Prix Corporation takes over the premises for the week of the race. They do pay the Club some compensation.

In 1998, at the instigation of Melbourne Parks and Waterways an arrangement was made with the Melbourne Petanque Club to share the premises. Parks Victoria had the boundaries of the area leased to the Bowling Club modified to allow two petanque *pistes* and a driveway to be constructed on the western boundary. They also paid for the construction of the *pistes* and the roadway. The western boundary of the Bowling Club's area had prior to this been three metres from the building. In 2000, lights were installed on the rear petanque *piste*, at a cost of $30,000. The Petanque group did not thrive, and the agreement with them was formally terminated in 2010. The petanque *pistes* were then used as car parks.

In the decade from 2005, the increasing revenue from corporate functions, and some grants from Government bodies, has funded an extensive program of capital improvements. Lights were added to the rear bowling green. Six 25,000 litre water tanks have been installed, and provide water for the toilets, and some of the water for the greens. All bowling greens have been converted to Tifdwarf. Both the men's and women's toilets have been rebuilt, and disabled toilet facilities added. A program of asphalting the car parks has been commenced, and the perimeter fences are progressively being replaced. The patio area has been re-roofed, and new sun shading installed. Extensive work on the western side of the 1955 building has improved its appearance considerably, and the bar storerooms have been upgraded.

Bowls

In Victoria the Pennant Competition is what bowls is all about. When Middle Park entered the Saturday Men's competition in 1905, there were 33 clubs, with sides in two divisions. Middle Park had sides in both divisions. The number of sides increased to four from 1920 to 1930; at this time Middle Park had as many sides as any club in Melbourne. The highest achievement possible is to win the Flag for the top level of competition. Middle Park won this in 1923, and went close on a number of other occasions. The numbers and the standard of play dropped off with the Depression in the 1930s, and did not pick up again until after the war. From 1946 until 1966, the Club had from six to eight pennant sides each year, with the top side in Division 1. The standard dropped off slightly after that, but there were at least five sides until 1987. From that time the numbers dropped significantly, as did the general standard, although there was always a core of good players. It is only since 2012 that the numbers have started climbing again, and the general standard improved. A coach has been employed since 2012.

There have always been individuals who achieved great things, particularly in the boom period between 1946 and 1966.

Bowls started in Australia as a gentleman's sport. Women did not play, although as 'Associate Members' they helped with fundraising and made the sandwiches. At Middle Park the women played from the start – although their use of the Men's Clubhouse was frowned on. From 1908 they had their own Clubhouse. A considerable expense, but obviously considered preferable to allowing the women into the men's domain. In 1906, the six clubs where women actually played formed the Victorian Ladies Bowling Association. The other five clubs involved were South Melbourne (in St Vincent's Place – it changed its name to Albert Park in 1929), the South Melbourne Cricket Club Bowling Club (which closed in 1979), Auburn, Brighton Beach, and Fitzroy (closed 1927). They started a pennant competition (playing on Tuesday) right away, for sides of eight people (two teams of four). The mid-week competition continues today, although it changed in 2002 from a competition for women only to an open competition. Middle Park has had at least one side in the competition every year, and is one of only four clubs to have done so. In the early years Middle Park did very well, and in fact dominated the competition, but there were very few clubs involved. By 1928 there were 23 clubs, the standard a lot higher, and Middle Park's era of dominance was over, although a good standard was maintained for quite some time.

There have since then been some individual champions. Eva Simpson won the Club Ladies Singles Championship 16 times, between 1922 and 1947. She won the VLBA Champion of Champions four times, in 1932, 1939, 1942 and 1945. No bowler in the history of the VLBA ever won more than four Champion of Champions. In more recent times Poppy Plumb won the Club Ladies Singles Championship 18 times between 1987 and 2008.

Finances

Bowling Clubs are generally incorporated as Not for Profit Associations. This means that any 'profits' from operations is spent on furthering the purposes of the Association, which is the promotion of lawn bowls. Over time, expenditure will be the same as income.

Traditionally, a bowling club's income comes from bar profits, members' subscriptions, fees for playing bowls, and sponsors. Historically, the Middle Park Bowling Club has spent most of its 'profits' on expanding and improving the premises. There were major efforts during the first 80 years.

1904	£300	Building the Green
1905	£150	Building the Clubhouse
1914	£400	Extensions to the Clubhouse
1918	£750	Construction of the Ladies Clubhouse, and the Greenkeeper's cottage.
1955	£13,000	Construction of a brick veneer extension.
1975	$35,000	Addition of locker rooms, replacement of weatherboards with imitation brick cladding, and renovation of the interior of the club building.
1982	$33,000	Replacement of the Ladies Clubrooms, and the Greenkeeper's cottage.
1985	$21,000	Refurbishment of the interior of the main building.

Major expenditures were in most cases financed by borrowing money (most commonly from members), and then repaying the loan out of income in succeeding years.

There was less major expenditure during the Club's period in the doldrums, from 1985 to 2005, although emphasis on cost control ensured there was always money in the bank.

In the last 10 years there has been a major change in the way the Club operates. The Club is now running a 'public green' where anyone can pay some money and play bowls. Many golf clubs have used this model for many years, but bowls clubs have traditionally seen themselves as exclusive private clubs. Perhaps this is a residue of the pre-World War II perception of bowls clubs as exclusive gentleman's clubs. In practice the major change has been hiring the clubhouse and the green for functions that involve playing bowls. The biggest group of such functions are company Christmas parties, involving some bowls, some drinking and some eating. The Club provides bowls and instruction, and people play in bare feet. This kind of operation involves substantial operating profits. The money has allowed the costs for members to play their game to be subsidised, and a new program of major expenditure, to bring the facilities up to standard. Between 2009 and March 2015, a total of $360,000 of Club money has been spent on improving the facilities – an average of $60,000 each year. The increased revenue has allowed this money to be paid each year from revenue, without having to borrow money.

Legal status

The Middle Park Bowling and Recreation Club commenced life as an unincorporated association. There were always difficulties in this status – the Club could not own property, so it was necessary to appoint 'trustees' who owned the property of the Club, and were limited by the Trust Deed as to what they could do with it. The Club as an entity could not sue or be sued, so anyone who thought they had been hard done by had to sue the Members of the Committee individually. Clubs could have incorporated under the Companies Act, but this was expensive and cumbersome, and involved quite onerous obligations.

In 1981 the Associations Incorporation Act made it very much easier for 'not for profit' groups to incorporate. The Middle Park Bowling Club was incorporated on 4 January 1990, although the Club was not restructured to reflect its new status until 1994. There was a Board of Management, and Men's and Ladies' Bowls sections. In April 2013 a new set of Rules was put in place, replacing the two bowls section with one, to reflect the fact that pennant competitions were now open, rather than Men's or Ladies' competitions.

The Bowling Club as a club

This chart shows the total number of members each year, the total number of people playing pennant, and the percentage of the total membership who played pennant. These figures show that right from the start, only about 40 per cent of the club members played bowls seriously. The club in fact had an additional function as a social club/community centre for its members. A number of people join each year to be part of this community, without intending to play bowls seriously.

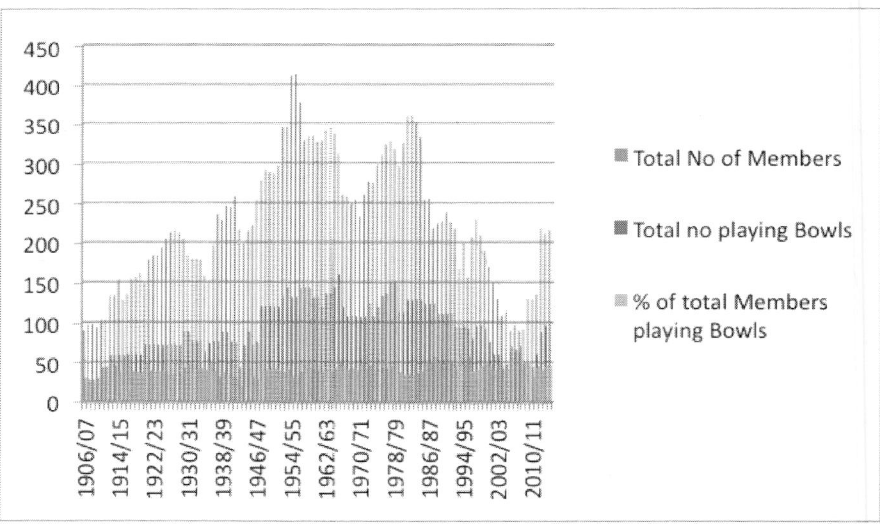

The group that the Club catered for changed over time. When the Club was formed in 1903, it was set up as a way for the local 'movers and shakers' to get together. The founding members saw themselves as important people. The first Chairman was George Elmslie, the local Member of Parliament, who was also involved in the formation of the South Melbourne Technical School, and was a President of the South Melbourne Football Club. In 1913 he formed a Government, becoming the first Labor Party Premier of Victoria. Tom Livingston was a foundation member, and remained a member until he died in 1922. His Parliamentary career included time as Minister for Public Instruction, and Minister for Mines and Forests. Solicitor George Godfrey was a Member of the Legislative Council , as was Tom Payne. Architect Tom Ashworth was a Member of the Legislative Assembly. A number of high status people were foundation members, but did not continue their membership after the first year. Clearly the founders wanted to give the impression that this was a high status club.

The initial annual subscription was two guineas (two pound two shillings), when the average weekly wage for an adult male was two pounds three and six and the average rent for a three-bedroom house was 13 shillings a week. Few poorer people could afford to be members. There were moves to keep out 'undesirables' – at a General Committee meeting on 25 August 1919, a motion was passed that 'bookmakers be not admitted as members of the Club'. Ironic that bookmaker and philanthropist Sol Green had been one of the founding members!

It is clear that many – perhaps most – bowling clubs founded in this era in Australia saw themselves as (slightly downmarket) versions of clubs such as the Melbourne Club, the Melbourne Cricket Club and the Victoria Racing Club. Victorians have always been fanatical about their sport, and bowls as a sport involves considerable skill and competitive spirit, and the physical demands are not beyond elderly gentlemen not in the best of physical condition. The game played in Australia was the version developed in Scotland in the second half of the 19th century, and since people from Scotland were over-represented in the ranks of the 'movers and shakers' of early Melbourne, it is not surprising that bowls developed as one of their main sporting interests.

Of course, bowling clubs were never serious competitors to high status clubs such as the Melbourne Club, the Australian Club or the Athenaeum. For a start they were generally established in the suburbs, and in the days before the rule of the motor car, they had essentially to draw on people who lived locally for their membership. Middle Park had been a middle class suburb from the start, so a bowling club in Middle Park was in a better position to survive as a relatively upmarket venture than clubs in most suburbs. It did well in this role until the Depression, but took quite a hit then. The number of members dropped, the income dropped, and the standard of bowls dropped. The Second World War, too, had quite an impact on the Club – much more than the First World War had had.

The club rooms were in fact taken over in 1942. The Army had an anti-aircraft gun emplacement in the park near the Clubhouse during 1942–43. It is believed the Army and AWAS (Australian Women's Army Service) personnel were stationed at the Club. Presumably the station was set up after the fall of Singapore, when there was a Japanese fleet with aircraft carriers in the Pacific, and there was concern that Melbourne could be attacked. The station would have been disbanded when it became clear that the Japanese navy was no longer a threat.

was maintained, and the percentage of them who bowled remained at about 40 per cent. The standard of bowls was maintained at a reasonable level until the mid 1980s. The Club was less successful from 1985, however, largely because the model that was being used to recruit new members didn't work anymore. The Club went into decline for 20 years. Performance on the bowling green mirrored this pattern.

Well-attired bowlers at Middle Park in the 1970s

In the period from 2005 the Club has re-invented itself, attracted a new group of members, and is now moving ahead on all fronts.

The Middle Park Bowling Club has always functioned partly as a bowling club, and partly as a social club/community centre for its members. The major conclusion that seems to emerge from considering its history is that whether it was going ahead or struggling as a bowling club at any particular time depended more than anything else on how well it was carrying out its social club/community centre function. The way the game of bowls was played has changed very little over its whole history. This has major implications for the way forward. Perhaps a good example of the value of the study of history.

MIDDLE PARK AND THE GREAT WAR

Edward Boyle

Federation

The early twentieth century was a period of great change nationally and locally. Prior to Federation the Australian colonies determined their own domestic policies, which included immigration and home defence. Britain controlled external affairs. The colony of Victoria had introduced legislation to restrict the entry of Chinese gold-seekers and had established a strong navy, forts around the bay and a system of voluntary part-time militias. The new Commonwealth Government now controlled immigration and defence. The 'White Australia Policy' was set in concrete with the Immigration Restriction Act (1901). A blue-water fleet, the Royal Australian Navy (RAN), was established and in 1910 compulsory military training for home defence was introduced following a tour and recommendations by Britain's Lord Kitchener. Other Western nations saw Australia as a 'social laboratory' with votes for women and pioneering welfare policies. Britain still controlled external affairs. Britain's declaration of war in August 1914 was binding on Australia.

Middle Park: old and new

While Emerald Hill and St Kilda were developing from the 1850s, and the heart of Albert Park from the 1860s, the Middle Park area was a swampy wasteland. The area was used for military purposes with the Emerald Hill Battery on the beach at the end of what became Kerferd Road and butts for small arms firing by members of part-time military units near the foreshore. Surveying, land sales, drainage and infrastructure works led to the boom period of the mid-1870s to early 1890s. There were visions of Middle Park rivalling the splendour of central Albert Park. Montalto, Hughenden, Lanark Terrace (demolished in controversial circumstances in the 1970s) and the Middle Park Hotel are some of the prime examples of the grand buildings of this boom period.

The boom, characterised by frenzied land speculation, turned to bust, with the collapse of numerous building societies. Development stalled for most of the 1890s. Post-depression development was largely of a different kind. As a young schoolgirl around 1914 Kathleen Pitt, the grand-daughter of John and Mary Buxton of Hughenden, and in adult life Associate Professor Kathleen Fitzpatrick in the History Department at Melbourne University, walked from her family's rented house at 68 Harold Street to her school in Albert Park, observing the new housing developments. In her memoir she recalled:

> ... building came to a standstill when the land boom burst. When it was resumed, at the turn of the century, the age of ostentation was over and Middle Park became a lower-middle class suburb, crowded with speculative builders' mean houses on minimal frontages, among which Grandpa's boom mansion was as incongruous as a ship stranded on dry land, alone.

One hundred years later she would have to eat her 'mean houses' words. And she ignored some gems, such as the graceful Italianate terraces next to Hughenden, built during the first decade and a half of the new century.

Hughenden in Beaconsfield Parade and row of
timber cottages in Wright Street

Kathleen Pitt/Fitzpatrick also recalled:

> … in our day the roads had not yet been sealed, and the wind perpetually whirled sand and dust along Harold Street … Our new neighbourhood was a lower-middle class district, chiefly inhabited by youngish couples like our parents, and it swarmed with children … The children of Harold Street were rough and sometimes a bit frightening. They used to roam the streets in packs, formed on a denominational basis, according to whether they went to State schools or Catholic primaries … children would chant: 'Catholic dogs (or 'Proddy' dogs)/ Jump like frogs/ In and out the water' …'

Sectarianism certainly reared its head during the conscription for overseas service referenda in October 1916 and December 1917. In her memoir Kathleen also recalled her delight when her father was promoted in the Treasury Department and able to pay a deposit on a spacious house in leafy, undulating East St Kilda, unlike the flat, dusty, treeless Middle Park in the infancy of its second stage of development.

Many of these new dwellings were obviously crowded houses. Back during the early twentieth century couples tended to have much larger families than a century later. Like the Pitts with their four children, it seems that many others lived in rented premises. Max Nankervis, in his chapter on Social Changes and Early Development in Middle Park, shows that owner-occupiers made up only about 38 per cent of the total. Landlords, many of whom lived in South Melbourne or St Kilda, typically owned several adjacent rental properties.

Who were the volunteers?

Presumably the rest of the Middle Park neighbourhood 'swarmed with children'. The older sons, like the Makin and Buxton brothers, were the ones who rushed to enlist beginning in August 1914. The World War I Honour Board at the South Melbourne Town Hall lists 2973 men out of an estimated population of 48,500. The former City of South Melbourne included Albert Park and Middle Park. Just how many were from the Middle Park area bounded by Kerferd Road and Fraser Street, Canterbury Road and Beaconsfield Parade is difficult to ascertain. So far some 150 local volunteers have been identified, enough to provide a representative sample. There are probably several hundred more yet to be identified. Outlines of the identified local volunteers, with links to their full military histories, can be found on the MPHG website under the *World War I* heading.

'In honour of the citizens of South Melbourne who fought in the Great War'

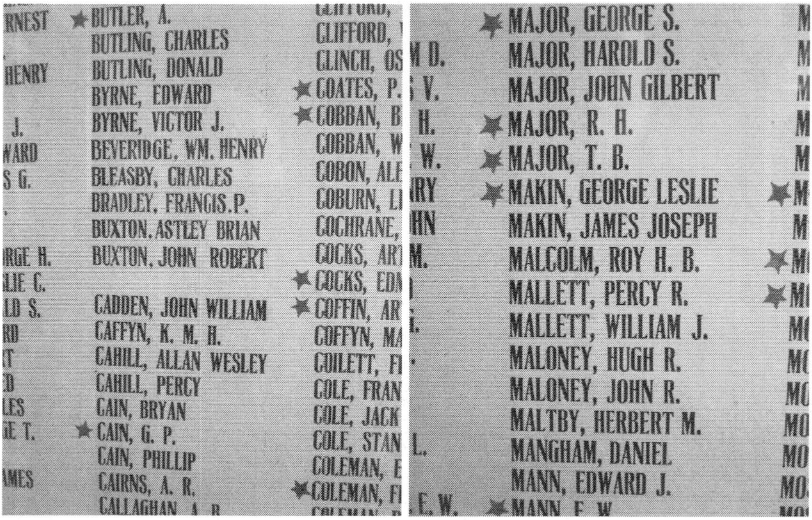

MIDDLE PARK: THE WAY WE WERE

RNEST ★BUTLER, A.
BUTLING, CHARLES
HENRY BUTLING, DONALD
BYRNE, EDWARD
J. BYRNE, VICTOR J.
WARD BEVERIDGE. WM. HENRY
S G. BLEASBY, CHARLES
BRADLEY, FRANCIS.P.
BUXTON.ASTLEY BRIAN
RGE H. BUXTON, JOHN ROBERT
LIE C.
LD S. CADDEN, JOHN WILLIAM
RD CAFFYN, K. M. H.
T CAHILL, ALLAN WESLEY
D CAHILL, PERCY
LES CAIN, BRYAN
E T. ★CAIN, G. P.
CAIN, PHILLIP
MES CAIRNS, A. R.
CALLAGHAN, A. R.

CLIFFORD,
CLIFFORD,
CLINCH, OS M D.
★COATES, P. V.
★COBBAN, B H.
COBBAN, W W.
COBON, ALE
COBURN, LI RY
COCHRANE, HN
COCKS, AR M.
★COCKS, EDM
★COFFIN, AR
COFFYN, MA
COILETT, F
COLE, FRAN
COLE, JACK
COLE, STAN L.
COLEMAN, E
★COLEMAN, F E. W.

★MAJOR, GEORGE S. M
MAJOR, HAROLD S. M
MAJOR, JOHN GILBERT M
★MAJOR, R. H. M
★MAJOR, T. B. M
★MAKIN, GEORGE LESLIE ★M
MAKIN, JAMES JOSEPH M
MALCOLM, ROY H. B. ★M
MALLETT, PERCY R. ★M
MALLETT, WILLIAM J. M
MALONEY, HUGH R. M
MALONEY, JOHN R. M
MALTBY, HERBERT M. MO
MANGHAM, DANIEL MO
MANN, EDWARD J. MO
★MANN, F. W. M

*The names of Astley and John Buxton and
Les and Jim Makin from the Honours Board*

Regarding age on enlistment, in round figures twenty were eighteen or nineteen years of age, one hundred were in their twenties, twenty were in their thirties, and ten in their forties. Most listed the name of a parent, a few a wife, living in the Middle Park area as next-of-kin. About ten gave the name of a parent living in England, Ireland, Scotland or New Zealand. Just over twenty were married and there were a few widowers. All but one listed a religious affiliation. In round figures, they were: sixty Church of England, thirty Roman Catholic, thirty Presbyterian, twenty Methodist, several Baptist or Church of Christ, and two of the Jewish faith. Regarding occupation, twelve listed a profession, including seven engineers. Twenty-five registered as clerks with the public service, shipping companies and the like. The overwhelming majority

154

gave occupations in the following categories: tradesmen, factory workers, salesmen or labourers. Middle Park was an ideal place for workers to rent or board, being close to the city and the then thriving industries of Port Melbourne and South Melbourne, reachable by 'shanks pony', bicycle or public transport.

The jobs of the majority of this sample at the time would have been seen as working-class occupations. This data indicates that Middle Park at the time was a mixture of working class and lower-middle class with pockets of solid middle class. The younger men were the ones who rushed to enlist. Most were assigned to the front-line infantry brigades. Older men were more likely to be assigned to support units such as medical, communications and transport units. The young men who enlisted early on were to face the carnage on Gallipoli during the latter two-thirds of 1915 and the even heavier losses at Fromelles and Pozieres in France in mid-1916. Married men as the breadwinners would have been reluctant to put their lives at risk. And before long knowledge of the pittance paid to war widows and their children would have become well known. When voluntary recruitment fell away the government offered the inducement of extra allowances to married men.

The combatants

The first campaign, during the latter third of 1914, was in the German colonies to Australia's north and north-east to disable the communications installations vital for German raiders in the Indian Ocean. William Higgie of 21 McGregor Street and several other locals fought in New Britain. Then the 1st Division and soon after the 2nd Division were sent to Egypt via the Suez Canal. During the latter two thirds of 1915 they fought at Gallipoli. After Gallipoli the survivors and new recruits were formed into four divisions, the 1st, 2nd, 4th and 5th Divisions. Later the 3rd Division was sent directly to England for the completion of training. As well there were mounted brigades which were to fight mainly in Palestine. The small Australian Flying Corps of three squadrons operated in the Middle East and in France. Some local volunteers transferred from the AIF to this corps. The RAN was placed under British control. From mid-1916 to late 1918 the infantry divisions fought on the Western Front around Armentieres in French Flanders and some eighty kilometres south in the Somme region. There are many fine histories of the battles in which Australians fought. In this account the war will be viewed through the experiences of several local combatants.

Cecil McAnulty

Cecil McAnulty

After completing his secondary education at the Jesuits' St Patrick's College in East Melbourne, Cecil Anthony McAnulty was employed as a clerk. At the age of twenty-seven and unmarried, he enlisted in November 1914. According to his military record, on the eve of embarkation he was discharged for being 'drunk in camp'. He re-enlisted and left for Egypt in May 1915. Then he was shipped to Gallipoli as part of the reinforcements for the 3rd Infantry Battalion. Imagine the anxiety of his parents, Cecilia and Paul McAnulty of

226 Richardson Street, as reports of heavy casualties on Gallipoli were published in the press.

Strategically, the Gallipoli campaign was planned to open up the sea route to Russia's Black Sea ports to support them in their battle against the Germans on the Eastern Front. The Dardanelles, the narrows from the Aegean to the Black Sea, had to be secured and Constantinople taken. The Allied warships in the face of Turkish mines and artillery failed to penetrate the Dardanelles. Troops were then allotted the doomed task of clearing the Turkish defences.

Private McAnulty kept two improvised diaries from 10 April 1915 to 8 August 1915 which have been preserved by the Australian War Memorial and are online. The diaries provide graphic details of the campaign:

> *Saturday 26th June.* Saw one of the most horrible sights I have ever seen, a man literally shot to pieces. The lad evidently had a machine gun turned on him at short range and there was hardly a square inch of his body that didn't have a bullet hole.

> *Sunday 8th August.* I'm all out, can hardly stand up. On Friday when we got the word to charge, Frank and I were on the extreme left of the charging party. There was a clear space of 100 yards to cross without a patch of cover. I can't realize how I got across it. I seemed to be in a sort of trance … We were right out in the open and all the Turkish machine guns and rifles seemed to be playing on us and shrapnel bursting right over us. I yelled to the other 4 chaps, 'This is only suicide, boys. I'm going to make a jump for it' …

This was Lone Pine. He was killed during the second week of August. There are no records of exactly how he met his death. He is buried at the Lone Pine Cemetery. Nine of the 150 identified local combatants were killed at Gallipoli. Afterwards it is likely his parents said to each other, or to themselves, 'If only Cecil had not re-enlisted.'

Les Makin

George Leslie Makin (left) with Captain Alasdair F. Gibson

George Leslie (Les) Makin of 91 Harold Street was the second oldest of Henry and Marianne Makin's six children. A strapping six-footer, Les was well above average height for the time; brother Jim was several inches taller again. Les had been a member of the 51st Regiment of the Citizens Forces at Albert Park for three years when war was declared. Only twenty years old, a Roman Catholic, single and a clerk, he enlisted immediately in August 1914. Assigned to the 5th Battalion, 2nd Brigade, 1st Division as Private Makin, he rose rapidly to the rank of lieutenant.

He was in the thick of the action from the beginning in April 1915 on Gallipoli. In early May his best mate was killed in the attack on strongly defended Krithia, Cape Helles. As he recalled in a letter of 26 January 1916 to his young brother Perce:

> You must tell people that I told you Vic Lusic died a brave man and a credit to Middle Park. Although I did not see him go down, I saw him a minute or two before and he was actually joking

about charging being good training for the ruck and the bullets were that thick overhead that if you had thrown your hat up it would have been riddled. Then we were up and off and while I only got a finger chipped, poor old Vic got two, either one of which would have killed him.

During August Les, like Cecil McAnulty, fought in the costly battle of Lone Pine. Soon after he was hospitalised on Lemnos suffering from enteric fever. From Lemnos in October he wrote to his brother Perce:

Two boys from Middle Park: Vic Lusic and Les Makin, in Egypt, on their way to Gallipoli.

… at the Lone Pine plateau, the bodies were so thick that for a week we had to walk on them, eat our meals and sleep among them. It was a real nightmare and several men broke down completely under the strain.

While convalescing in England he wrote home:

Dear Mother (7–2–1916) I am one of the luckiest men in the world today. When I think, how I was on the Peninsular for five months & am alive to write about it I cannot but marvel, for every square foot of ANZAC was at one time or another swept with fire … luck was with me when I needed it most.

As he recovered he was able to attend the theatre in London and enjoy time as a guest at country estates. He also experienced Zeppelin bombing attacks on London. In May he was passed fit to return to the front. Like his brother Jim he fought in the costly battle of Pozieres/Mouquet Farm north-east of Amiens from late July to early August 1916. In a letter home dated 20 November 1916 he told his family that at Pozieres as a result of exploding shells he had been buried three times in one night. In May 1917 he was in charge of his company during the Second Battle of Bullecourt north-east of Pozieres.

Les Makin (standing far right) with nurses in London 1916

In September 1917 he was hospitalised again suffering from trench fever, a debilitating bacterial infection resulting from the exposed, unhygienic conditions in the trenches. A letter to brother Perce dated 25 March 1918 describes another horror of the war:

The latest gas they (the Germans) have used not only affects the lungs but burns the flesh anywhere it comes in contact. Up in Wandsworth Hospital at this moment are 12 to 14 Australian officers. A week ago they were fine strong men. Today they are dying in agony. Ghastly to look upon, for their eyes have been burnt out and noses and hands eaten away by acid.

Both sides used gas as a weapon. Drawing on his experiences as a German soldier on the Western Front, Erich Remarque gave a graphic account of what it was like to be on the receiving end of a gas attack in his novel *All Quiet on the Western Front*. Les instructed Perce not to show their mother letters dealing with the horrors of the war.

Family photograph of Les Makin (second from right) on convalescent leave in London before returning to the battlefront in France.

In mid-1918 Les was reunited with his battalion. Under General Monash the Australians played a key role in stopping the German advance on Amiens. The Allies then counter-attacked, driving the Germans back to the Hindenburg Line. At this stage the Americans had their baptism of fire. Lieutenant Makin was leading his company in the counter-offensive. At Bray-sur-Somme, halfway between Amiens and Mont St Quentin, he suffered severe injuries to both legs when struck by a shell. For two weeks he battled for his life in the 8th General Hospital in Rouen. It was difficult to control infection and his right leg was amputated. He died on 8 September, nine weeks before the Armistice.

He is buried in the St. Sever Cemetery, Rouen, France. In an online tribute Joanne Scanlan, whose grandmother was Les's sister, notes that his portrait still holds pride of place on the wall of the family's Harold Street home.

Jim Makin in the Middle Park CYMS Cricket Club 1921, and as a VFL footballer 1923

Jim Makin

James (Jim) Joseph Makin, also of 91 Harold Street, was the third eldest of the six children. He enlisted in August 1915 and embarked from Port Melbourne in February 1916 on the troopship Warilda. He recorded the scene in his diary:

As strand after strand of the paper streamers broke and the boat slowly drew out from the pier, many

mothers gave way and wept, and not a few of our hardiest lads showed signs of emotion. I myself felt a strange feeling creep over me as I watched the thousands of mothers, wives, sisters and sweethearts earnestly gazing at and waving to some dear one on board.

Of course, those farewelling these volunteers knew that some 8000 similar men had already been killed during the Gallipoli campaign.

Troopship Warilda departing Port Melbourne, February 1916

Jim Makin was assigned to the 21st Battalion, 6th Brigade, 2nd Division. He had his baptism of fire in the costly battle of Pozieres in the Somme region. One of the last entries in his diary was 28th July 1916:

What a night! I shall never forget the sights as long as I live. It was one nightmare. The decomposed bodies of the unburied dead, the shattered bodies of those just killed by shells, and the badly wounded being carried back was sufficient to unnerve the strongest.

Thereafter he discontinued his diary. From the County of London War Hospital he wrote to his young brother Perce on 7 August:

> I daresay by the time you receive this note you will have heard that I am in England recovering from the shock caused by one of Fritz's high explosive shells bursting alongside me … I regard myself as a very lucky man indeed. Almost the whole of my platoon and company were either killed or wounded before I was buried. I seemed to have a charmed life for many times a shell killed and wounded men on both sides of me and pieces of shell case missed by inches. I was ready for death at any moment but I was spared.

Les and Jim Makin finally met up in England after the Battle of Pozieres. Over the next two years there were further meetings during which the brothers made plans to go on the land, although Jim wrote to their mother that he thought he was more suited to working with his head than with his hands.

As he recovered Jim was assigned to clerical work in England. He was selected in the AIF's rugby team for the grudge match against the Welsh Guards; the AIF won. He was finally promoted to the rank of sergeant. Before he was considered fit to return to the front the Armistice was signed. He returned to Australia in January 1919. Not quite in his mid-twenties, he went on to play thirty games with South Melbourne and sixteen with Melbourne in the VFL. Then he left to live abroad. According to his nephew Perce Makin (son of Perce), he established a successful concreting business in Hawaii. Apparently he later moved to California where he died in 1977.

The Makin brothers meet up in London when both had been invalided back to England. Jim Makin, second from left; Les Makin, right. Alisdair F. Gibson, a medical officer, also seen in a previous photograph with Les Makin, is between the brothers. Les Makin would return to France and die a few months later.

Jack and Astley Buxton

John and Mary Buxton had nine children: four daughters and five sons. John Buxton was a successful real estate agent and a pioneer of Middle Park. He built his grand mansion, Hughenden, on Beaconsfield Parade near Mills Street around 1890. John (Jack)

Robert Buxton enlisted in August 1914 and embarked soon after in October as a private in the 5th Battalion, 2nd Brigade, 1st Division. Jack's second youngest brother, the debonair Astley Brian Buxton, popularly known as 'Ack', enlisted later and embarked in June 1915 as a member of the 6th Field Ambulance.

Jack's niece, the one who became an historian, wrote in her memoir:

> Poor uncle Jack, his luck was out, as usual, in the war. He never rose from the ranks, he was never wounded or invalided, he just had to sweat it out. The whole dreadful promiscuousness and sordidness of life as a private in the infantry of the tough AIF, all through the Gallipoli campaign and later, in the trenches in France, was sheer torture to a terribly thin-skinned man.

His official military records belie some of these impressions. He was in fact promoted to lance-sergeant and, although apparently it was not granted, he was recommended for the high honour of the Military Medal for '... personal bravery and good work as runner at Pozieres.' As a Gallipoli veteran he was one of the first to be repatriated on the principle of 'first in first out'. With few exceptions returned servicemen like Jack would not talk openly to non-combatants about their war experiences. His niece's memoir points to the aftermath:

> When he came home, at last, we thought he would enjoy sleeping in a proper bed, but for months he could only sleep on the floor … as the years went on he drank to shut out his memories of the horrors and the carnage he had been unlucky enough to live through.

Astley Buxton's registration details were: twenty-one, Roman Catholic, clerk and single. He enlisted in February 1915 and embarked in June. He was a private in the 6th Field Ambulance and then the 12th Field Ambulance. Like so many of his fellow soldiers, he suffered from a variety of injuries and illnesses and was hospitalised several times. His military file shows that he suffered chronic synovitis of the right knee, jaundice and severe abscesses. He returned to Australia in November 1917 and was discharged in March 1918. In March 1918 he was granted a war pension. Astley died, comparatively young, in 1939. It seems likely that his health had been permanently affected during his war service. According to Kathleen Fitzpatrick, the youngest brother, Len, tried to enlist but was rejected on medical grounds.

John Buxton (uncle Jack) in France

Astley Brian Buxton (left) and John Robert Buxton (right)

The home front

An army of 417,000 was raised out of a population of almost 5 million. Over 330,000 of these served overseas. In total 58,132 servicemen died and 156,228 were gassed, wounded or taken prisoner. Tens of thousands of people back home endured years of anxiety, many grieving. Hundreds of people in Middle Park would have been receiving letters, like the Makins, detailing the horrors of the new industrialised warfare. Women and children did their bit to support the men, and some women as nurses, who went away to war too. Lillian Helen Nuzum of 85 Wright Street was one of the 2139 women who served overseas with the Australian Army Nursing Service.

Busy Bee Wagon c. 1916

Based at Port Melbourne, the Swallow and Ariel's Busy Bees wagon was a regular sight in South Melbourne, Albert Park and Middle Park, encouraging young men to enlist and others to donate money for comforts for the men abroad. Typical of the many groups providing support was the local Methodist Church's branch of the Red Cross League. ANZAC biscuits and socks, hundreds of them, were to be found in the parcels they, and others, sent overseas. Why so many socks? The trenches were water-logged for much of the year, as Les Makin described in a letter to Perce in November 1916: 'Conditions here are rather trying. Rain every day and cold as charity. Mud up to the waist and I haven't been dry for a fortnight.' Changing socks regularly helped prevent foot rot, which could be crippling. School children raised money and girls knitted, yes, mainly socks. Many local girls attended the Brigidine Sisters' Kilbride College on Beaconsfield Parade, Albert Park. They raised money to send to nuns in Belgium who cared for civilian victims of war.

There were local manifestations of divisions in Australian society, in particular on the treatment of those of German heritage and over the issue of conscription for overseas service. Some zealots victimised German Australians; others decried the unfounded accusations against them. There was a local branch of the Anti-German League. Its members were not necessarily zealots. The local paper, the *Record* (27 May 1916), reported an example of its welfare work. At the reported meeting the members voted to support a war widow with two children by helping her to set up a small business. Her husband had been killed at Gallipoli.

Australians were deeply divided on the issue of conscription for overseas service. With the decline of voluntary enlistment Prime Minister Billy Hughes was anxious to keep up the strength of the Australian divisions which were suffering heavy losses. He wanted to ensure a strong voice at the eventual peace settlement. In particular he was worried that Japan might claim the German colonies to Australia's near north and north-east.

His Labor Party was mainly against conscription. The first referendum (technically a plebiscite) in October 1916 failed narrowly. He left the ALP to lead non-Labor. The national debate prior to the second referendum (plebiscite) of December 1917 was even more acrimonious. Women were to the fore in both the 'Yes' and 'No' camps. Many local boys attended the Christian Brothers' College in St Kilda. Their speech-night was to be held on the eve of the referendum. Archbishop Mannix, originally from Ireland, who was advocating a 'No' vote, was to be the guest speaker at the St Kilda Town Hall. The 1916 Irish Easter Uprising had been ruthlessly crushed by the British. At the eleventh hour a majority of councillors ruled that the booking would be cancelled if Archbishop Mannix was not withdrawn from his engagement. Instead the speech-night was held at the college with a large crowd waving banners supporting Irish Independence and advocating a 'No' vote. Many members of the strong Our Lady of Mount Carmel parish in Middle Park attended. The December referendum also failed narrowly.

Aftermath of war

John Grant, a member of the Imperial Camel Corps, was killed during the Battle of Romani in mid-1916. Here the Allies stopped an attempt by the enemy to cut off the vital supply route of the Suez Canal. No details of how he died and where he was buried were recorded. His file shows that Ethel, his wife, of 25 Nimmo Street, received the base war widows' pension, with allowances for her two children, David and Winifred. The combined amount was below the basic wage. In July 1919 she applied for assistance under the War Service Home Act. She was asked to provide a marriage certificate. Much later in December 1935, when she had moved to Sydney, presumably to be with supportive relatives, the War

Service Commission asked her to provide documentation on her late husband's war service. The file does not show whether or not Ethel finally received assistance to buy a home. On top of the pain of loss, war widows without private means faced years of financial hardship. By contrast American war widows received substantial compensation.

Les Makin instructed his young brother Perce not to show their mother his letters detailing the horrors of war. Imagine her pain on receiving news of his death so close to the end of the war. Robert Murray Lister, from 6 Mills Street, was killed in July 1916 during the disastrous attack at Fromelles and has no known grave. His file has copies of requests by his parents to various authorities for information about what had happened to their son. The documents also show that Robert's parents, John and Matilda, left Melbourne to live in England in mid-1919. Perhaps it was to be near where their beloved son had met his fate. It is likely they visited the battle field in France. If so, they would have seen their son's name on the commemorative wall at the V.C. Corner Memorial, Fromelles.

> *Every bullet has its billet,*
> *Some bullets more than one.*
> *For you sometimes kill a mother,*
> *When you kill a mother's son.*

Joseph Lee

This writer has not been able to find any studies on how the children of the war dead were affected. Being told their fathers were patriotic war heroes would not necessarily have eased confused emotions. Children could not fully grasp why their mothers were so deeply traumatised. Several years after the end of the war ex-servicemen formed Legacy. From the mid-1920s they focused on the children of their fallen comrades – the Junior Legatees. They acted as mentors and ran gymnastics classes and holiday camps and provided educational assistance. As adults many of these children, and other descendants, have conducted research to find out what really happened to their forebears. The archival work of Perce Makin and Maree Wilson has been invaluable for this chapter.

Australian troops were well trained and equipped, and effective. Their military exploits are proudly honoured. More than 150,000 Australian troops suffered wounds, gassing and war-related illnesses. There is a stark reminder in George Johnston's *My Brother Jack*. He drew on childhood memories. His mother was a repatriation nurse who brought home amputees for a break from hospital. One guest had lost both arms and legs. There is a growing interest and concern about the long-term psychological effects of war. The case studies here point to the horrors of war. As Les Makin wrote to his brother about Lone Pine, '… several men broke down completely under the strain.' Lt. Col. Dave Grossman, psychology professor at West Point, has surveyed and analysed the scholarly research on Post-traumatic Stress Disorder (PTSD). Armies program soldiers to kill fellow human beings, which is against the innate nature of most people. The more immediate the killing (artillerymen kill at a distance) the more traumatic the effects, short-term and/or long-term. For the infantry of the Great War the killing was immediate, vicious ('Fix bayonets!') and relentless, as demonstrated in the case studies. Many, like Jim Makin, suffered 'shell shock', which is now recognised as PTSD. Kathleen Fitzpatrick's observations about her uncle, Jack Buxton, suggest long-term PTSD. Grossman argues that most of the combatants of the Great War almost certainly suffered long-term psychological costs, that is PTSD.

Recently a Salvation Army grief counsellor, commenting on the cycle of grief (shock, denial, anger, acceptance and closure), observed in an interview that there is never really full closure. Scott Bennett in *Pozieres: the Anzac story* gives examples of parents, especially mothers, seeking information about the fate of their sons long after the war had ended. For a high percentage of those killed there was no information on just how they were killed and where they were buried – 'An Australian Soldier of the Great War Known Unto God'.

'Known Unto God'

Albert Park's Lambis Englezos understands inter-generational grief. In 1992 he helped found the Friends of the 15th Brigade. This brigade was part of the 5th Division which fought in the disastrous Battle of Fromelles. Through this organisation he befriended several veteran diggers who recounted the grim realities of the battle. On a visit to Fromelles in 2002 he suspected that some of the troops of the 5th Division slaughtered in that battle were buried by the Germans in a collective grave which had not been found at the end of the war.

His research, with a small team of supporters, led him to conclude that an unearthed collective grave was probably adjacent

Lambis Englezos at Fromelles

to Pheasant Wood near the village of Fromelles. In 2007 a non-intrusive examination of the site indicated it was very likely the site of a mass grave. The next year an intrusive archaeological investigation confirmed his 2002 hypothesis.

During 2009 the remains of 250 soldiers were recovered. They were reburied with full military honours in a new commemorative cemetery near the Pheasant Wood site. DNA testing, as well as examination of dental records, associated artefacts and the like, have led to 150 of the Australian soldiers being identified. Hundreds of descendants attended the centenary service at Fromelles in July 2016. Thanks primarily to Lambis, so far 150 Australian soldiers are no longer only 'Known Unto God'. Two of the Middle Park soldiers known to have been killed at Fromelles, Herbert Evan Jones and Robert Murray Lister, still have no known grave.

Ceremony at Pheasant Wood Cemetery, Fromelles, 19 July 2016 attended by hundreds of descendants of the Australian soldiers who had died 100 years ago.

THE GREEK IMMIGRANTS OF MIDDLE PARK

Introduction by Sonya Cameron

Oral interviews by Anne Miller

Introduction: the background to Greek immigration

When we think of the large Greek immigration to Australia, particularly Victoria, in the 1950s and 1960s, we forget that many Greeks migrated to Victoria a century earlier. Greek migrants from the Ionian Islands (which was a British Protectorate from 1815–1864) arrived in the 1850s to make their fortune in the gold rush and then planned to return to Greece once they had amassed some wealth. In a portent of what was to happen 100 years later, most never returned and instead settled in New South Wales and Victoria. However, as they were mostly bachelors, over time they married local girls and assimilated into the local community. Gradually the number of Greek immigrants increased, mainly due to the chain migration of families from the Greek Islands. Then, in the 1920s, following the Asia Minor Catastrophe and the new restriction on immigrants imposed by the United States, migration from the Greek mainland began. These later immigrants were unable to find employment in urban areas and were forced to work in isolated rural areas. Far from home and families and with inadequate language skills they suffered health and mental problems. But despite these early setbacks, more and more Greek immigrants arrived and began settling in the urban areas. Migrants from the same family or village lived together in crowded communes in order to support each other and to retain their traditions, values and customs. They also appreciated the good education available to their children and the ability to acquire wealth, particularly through the purchase of real estate, to provide themselves with financial security. Because chain migration brought together settlers from the same village or region a plethora of local societies developed to protect their local customs from foreigners – these being not the Australians but rather those from other Greek regions. One such society formed in Middle Park was the Lemnian Brothers Club which purchased the former Middle Park Theatre in 1981 and used the premises for their meetings.

Following World War II chain migration was replaced by mass migration. Australia felt vulnerable to attack from the north due to its low population which was exacerbated by the low birth rate. The new migrants could also provide skilled and unskilled workers to stimulate economic growth. It was during this period that Arthur Calwell coined the phrase 'populate or perish' and whose immigration policies have had such a profound effect on the shaping of Australia. Following the establishment of the Immigration Department in 1945 the first 'assisted immigration scheme' agreements were made, with Italy and Malta. A similar agreement with Greece was signed in 1952. Greek migration to Australia peaked in 1964–65 but then declined dramatically following the restoration of democracy to Greece in 1974 and the improvement in economic conditions in Greece. Moreover, many Greek immigrants began to return to Greece to live. But in that period 250,000 migrants from Greece and Cyprus had arrived in Australia. In the 1971 census 160,000 persons stated that they were born in Greece, of whom forty-seven per cent lived in Melbourne. They tended to live in the inner suburbs of Melbourne and, in the suburb of South Melbourne, four per cent of the population were Greek. Later census data specifically for Middle Park shows a now declining number of residents who were born in Greece – due no doubt to an ageing Greek population. In 2001 it was still around the four per cent mark with 4.2% of Middle Park residents born in Greece, in 2006 it was 3.8% and in 2011 3.2%. But despite the decline in the numbers of the original immigrants, it appears that their children have not moved away. The 2011 Census records that 8.4% of residents of Middle Park claimed Greek heritage, the largest migrant group in the suburb, and a percentage that has hardly changed in the last ten years (9.6% in 2001).

Most of the Greek migrants were initially unskilled young men from urban areas or the impoverished rural areas, with limited education. But they worked hard to establish themselves in their new country which gave them plenty of opportunities to do so. Like the inter-war Greek migrants they lived together in crowded residences in order to save money to later buy a place of their own. Due to their limited English and lack of skills the type of work available to them was mainly on the production lines of large manufacturers, such as the car industry and food processing factories, or on sewing machines in the textile and footwear factories. There was also a severe gender imbalance due to the lack of Greek women with whom they could socialise (marriage between a Greek male and a non-Greek woman was frowned on by the conservative Anglo-Saxon population). At the time the Greek government discouraged the migration of unmarried Greek women. The problem was partially solved in 1954 with the Australian government promising to help with their settlement but it was not until 1961 that the Greek government allowed the unrestricted emigration of unmarried women.

For this new post-World War II wave of Greek immigrants it was important to them to maintain their cultural and social heritage along with their faith and their language. To this end they tended to migrate to suburbs where earlier Greek immigrants were already settled as a way of maintaining their identity as Greeks – new migrants were expected to assimilate into the Australian way of life and even Anglicise their names. It was not until the Whitlam Government came to power in 1972 that the policy of assimilation began to be questioned. Their dismantling of the White Australia Policy was the first step in recognising the rights of immigrants to express and share their cultural identity. In 1973, the Minister for Immigration, Al Grassby, gave a speech entitled a 'Multicultural Society for Australia' in which the term 'multiculturalism' was used for the first time – a term that was borrowed from the Canadians. This new policy was followed and improved by Whitlam's successors – Malcolm Fraser, Bob Hawke and Paul Keating until it became entrenched in the Australian way of life.

The three stories on the following pages are from Greek migrants living and working in Middle Park – two from women who migrated from Greece and one from a local businessman whose parents migrated from Greece but he was born in Australia and works in Middle Park. Their stories will provide an insight as to why they left their homeland and describe how they have settled in their new homeland.

Interviews with residents who came from Greece in the 1960s

Calliopi Fonias

Calliopi Fonias interviewed at her home in Harold Street by Anne Miller on 25 September 2015.

Sonya Cameron, also from the Middle Park History Group and who knows Calliopi, was present.

My early life in Greece

I was born in 1942 in Petra, a small village of about 800 people on the island of Lesbos (Lesvos). My family was comprised of my parents, an older brother and myself. My grandmother lived nearby and I have her name. This name is continued with my granddaughter here in Australia.

Calliopi on her wedding day

The family were farmers, initially growing tobacco plants. This was very hard work getting up about 4 am to collect the tobacco leaves and then going under the shade to thread the leaves using needles and string so that they could be placed in the sun to dry. When the leaves were dry they were packed on pallets and people from Athens would come to check the quality. If the leaves were of good quality the family would be paid but, if not, the leaves would be burned. This was very hard for my parents growing the crop for the whole year but not knowing until the last minute if it would be acceptable. Later my father became a vegetable farmer growing tomatoes, eggplants and beans. This was still a hard life but more successful. Summer time was OK growing the vegetables but in winter, except for leeks and spinach, vegetables did not provide sufficient income. If we purchased items from the grocery store they had to fill in an official piece of paper listing what we had spent so that in the summer when we were making money we could pay off these bills, but we could not pay day by day or week by week. This required trust by the shopkeeper. My father was a very hard worker. On the farm we also had animals – goats, chickens for eggs, and one cow for milk which enabled us to make butter and cheese. On special days we would kill a chicken to cook it. We also grew olives which were taken to a factory in the village where we were paid according to the weight and the oil was pressed. Our family did not grow grapes for wine but other families in the village did.

My parents were keen for my brother and myself to better ourselves by having a good education. So my brother became a qualified electrician after attending the school in Mitilini. I completed primary school and then high school for six years and I wanted to become a teacher. But because some of the villagers accused my father of being a Communist, I was failed in my entrance examination for teaching. Very soon after this I met my future husband. At high school I had learned English. After I left school, from the age of eighteen to when I was twenty-two I joined a group in the village learning to read and write English.

Coming to Australia

I have been the only one in my family to emigrate to Australia. I had met my future husband Michael, who was a motor mechanic, in Petra. Because we did not want the hard life of our parents Michael suggested that we go to Australia for seven years and then return to Greece. Michael and I were engaged before we left Greece. At the time of our engagement Michael did not like my long hair so he took me to Mitilini to a hairdresser to have it cut short! Our decision to come to Australia and to Melbourne was influenced by Michael's brother having already migrated to Melbourne. Michael travelled to Australia in 1962, coming to Melbourne where his brother and mother had arrived earlier. He then organised the paperwork for me to join him on 20 January 1964 travelling on the *Ellinis* by myself on its first trip to Australia. When the ship arrived at Station Pier I went to the home of my future brother-in-law and sister-in-law, living also with my future mother-in-law and my future husband. The brother-in-law's name is Alex; his house is at 379 Montague Street, Albert Park where he still lives today.

I started work at a factory off Montague Street near Ferrars Street where they made the radiators for cars. I was taught the job at the factory. There were many other Greek people working there too, and I found the work hard. Initially Michael had not been able to get work but he did get a position at General Motors, Dandenong and later at Preston Motors, Russell Street, Melbourne.

I marry Michael Fonias

On 30 August 1964 Michael and I were married at the Greek Orthodox church of St. Constantinos & St. Helen in Prahran. This church subsequently burned down but was rebuilt. It was disappointing for me that my parents could not be here for my wedding but my brother-in-law was present. My own brother came to Australia considerably later when our son was married in 1990. Our wedding was similar to what I might have had in Greece but with a smaller party after the church ceremony, held at Alex's house. Here we had spanokopita, meat balls with sauce and salads. There were other people from Petra at the wedding who now live in Melbourne.

Michael and I continued to live with Michael's brother until 1966. Michael was working very hard as a motor mechanic, he also fixed people's cars. I was also working hard as I would accept any offers from my employees for overtime work. My mother-in-law was very helpful as she did a lot of the cooking and other domestic work.

Our family

Once in Australia I continued my English lessons through the radio. I was sent the requisite books and every morning I would listen to the radio, complete the lesson and send it to the teacher. I am uncertain whether this facility was only for Greek people or for all migrants. In the early days after my arrival we were mainly mixing with Greek-speaking people whom we met through my brother-in-law and sister-in-law. Many of these people were from Petra.

In 1966 Michael and I moved to the house in which I live today. Michael's mother moved to Harold Street with us too. She looked after the domestic chores. Our first son, Christopher, was born in November 1965 before we moved to Harold Street. He is named after my father. Our second son was born in 1971, he is named Duke after Michael's father.

Following Christopher's birth I returned to work at the radiator factory and my mother-in-law looked after the baby. At the factory, National Radiators, the radiator-making section moved to another location while the factory in Montague Street changed to making nozzles and the spring for hair-spray containers. The factory also made the plastic parts. By this time I was in charge of quality control which was largely thanks to my good grasp of English. I stayed at this factory, N.C.L. Precision Products Pty Ltd, for a long time, I did not like changing jobs. But eventually the factory moved to Mount Waverley which is a long way from Middle Park and difficult for me to get to as at this time I did not drive. Because I was a good and consistent worker as a Supervisor of quality control my employers tried to persuade me to continue. Eventually they organised for a man in the accounts department of the factory who lived in St. Kilda to take me to and from the factory each day in his car. Michael would drive me to St. Kilda and I would be brought back to Middle Park after work. This was a new factory making the hair-spray fittings but employing mainly Australian people. I stayed here until I was pregnant with my second child in 1971. Following Duke's birth I found a job at Swallow and Ariel, biscuit manufacturers in Port Melbourne, after hearing an advertisement on the radio. Here I was also involved in the quality control, monitoring the colour of the biscuits, checking the weight of the ingredients and making a report. I liked this job.

As my mother-in-law spoke little English, in the house the family spoke Greek.

Other family members here and in Greece

My father wanted to come to Melbourne when I was ready to return to Petra forever, but he became sick in 1979 and subsequently died. In 1982 I returned to Petra to bring my mother to Melbourne to live here with me and my family. She came in 1982 and stayed here until 1989. At this time my mother-in-law was living with us too which did not prove to be easy, so eventually my mother-in-law returned to living with Alex, her other son in Albert Park.

My mother went back to Greece in 1989 but was not happy. In 1990 when Christopher was to be married she and my brother came back to Australia. In 1993 my mother became sick again and died. I then took her back to Greece to bury her in Petra. My mother-in-law died in 1997.

Kindergarten and schooling

Christopher attended the Middle Park kindergarten in Mills Street next to the primary school. When I worked at Swallows, Michael would take Christopher to school and my mother-in-law looked after the baby.

Christopher and Duke both attended the Middle Park Primary School. Through their contact with the school the Fonias family got to know more Australian families. Because Michael and I were keen for our children to have a good education both boys continued their secondary schooling at Wesley College on St. Kilda Road. Here there were very many fewer Greek children at the school – only one in Christopher's class. At Wesley Christopher and Duke were involved with rowing on the Yarra River. They are not involved with rowing now.

They also went to the local beach and swam with their friends. Once the boys were at school Michael and I made the decision to stay in Australia, partly because the children were fitting in very well at the school and it did not seem like a good idea to make the upheaval and take them back to Greece.

Duke, Calliopi, Christopher and Michael Fonias, 1990

Shopping

Michael and I did our shopping mainly at the South Melbourne market but purchased our groceries at the supermarket in Armstrong Street. Now I do most of my shopping at the market. In the early 1970s I commenced work at a delicatessen at the South Melbourne market. Here they started work at 5.30 am and as the trams had not commenced running at this hour, the proprietor of the business organised a taxi to collect me and the four other employees. In 1992 the owner of the Picadeli delicatessen shop at the market asked me to help her. I still help there when needed.

Impressions of Middle Park

When I came to live in Middle Park it reminded me of my village in Greece as I was able to see the sea each day. When we were looking for a house we wanted to be near the beach. Also it was quiet and things were convenient, close to the beach, shops and the city. At the time of purchase some friends suggested to me that the house was small but I think that having all these attractions and facilities nearby suits me well.

The family in 2015

Presently Duke and his family are living in Ormond. Christopher was married and divorced and now lives with me. Christopher's son, Michael, lives with his mother but comes to Harold Street every second weekend. Right now (at the time of the interview) Michael, who is named after his grandfather, is staying in Middle Park for three weeks as his mother is in Spain on holiday. I think that my sons have been more successful in their careers than they would have been if they had been brought up in Petra.

Returning to Greece

In 1976 Michael finished working at Preston Motors and the family travelled to Greece for six months. On his return a friend asked him to join him in running a petrol station and car workshop in Barkly Street St. Kilda. This was hard work as they were open 12 hours each day for 7 days of the week.

Michael died in August 2007.

Aris Yiannakis

Aris Yiannakis interviewed in August 2015 at the home of Anne Miller in Middle Park. Aris, whose birth name is Aristides, one of the early Greek philosophers, lives with his family in Brighton. He conducts a shoe repair business at 3B Armstrong Street, Middle Park.

My parents' early life in Greece

My forebears lived on the island of Lemnos in the Aegean Sea. My grandfather wasn't born on the island but he had a farm there and he also ran a shop in which my father and his brothers worked. My father had a donkey that he walked around the island, selling produce to the other islanders. In 1960 my father heard that the Australian government was encouraging Greek people to come to Australia to work. Thousands of young Greek men, including my father, boarded ocean liners such as the *Patris* and came to Station Pier in Melbourne. Some of these immigrants then went on to Bonegilla, others to South Australia and others to stay with family members already in Australia.

Aris outside his current shop at 3B Armstrong Street

My mother met my father in Melbourne. She had also grown up on a farm on Lemnos and came to Melbourne with a group of women from the island. In those days in Melbourne many people from the one community or from one of the islands back in Greece had gatherings in Melbourne, which was how my parents met each other; they did not know each other back on Lemnos. When my father left the island there was a depression in Greece and no work; the incentive for coming to Australia was the opportunity to work and money offered by the government to get settled here. Further back in the history of Lemnos the island had been occupied at various times by Turkey and then by Greece, and some people living on the island were really refugees. My father, like his father, had not been born on Lemnos, rather in Mosconisi in Turkey. I don't think either of my parents had been to school on the island

and today my mother still cannot read or write English. My father is no longer alive.

Father's arrival in Australia

My father first worked in South Australia at one of the vineyards/wineries but decided that he did not like this type of work. On arrival in Melbourne, he was taken in by one of his relatives who had previously arrived here, purchased a house and taken in fellow nationals in shared rooms until such time as they could buy their own houses. From here these new arrivals spread out to other places, met women or were 'matchmaked' into a relationship. Sometimes they would go to dances in Lonsdale Street, or certainly meet up with other immigrants from Lemnos. Father's first job in Melbourne in 1966 was as a labourer when the St. Kilda Junction was being re-profiled from eight intersecting streets into its present format. Later he worked, together with a group of Greek people, for Australian Gypsum (now Boral) in Oakleigh making plasterboard. This was at a time when the sheets were made and installed manually. In his later fifties Father went to work at the large complex of the Montefiore Jewish Home in Punt Road as a gardener and cleaner. After this position he retired. My father was a hard worker who established himself well here, but never in the bootmaking business. Together with three uncles he set up various businesses in properties and apartments.

Mother's arrival in Australia

I think when my mother arrived in Melbourne she was involved in domestic work for other people. And later she worked at the Montefiore Home as a maid.

My parents' marriage

My parents' marriage was celebrated at St. Dimitrios' Greek Orthodox Church in High Street, Prahran. Following the service they had their photographs taken at a studio where the background was of the gondolas in Venice! Their marriage was celebrated with a meal and the following day they both went to their respective workplaces. Following their marriage the Yiannakis family lived in Prahran and they did later move to Inkerman Street, North Caulfield. I remember that at one time when my father returned from work he was feeling very lethargic and weak and this worried my mother who tried to remedy the situation by feeding him more sweet foods! When my father went to the hospital he was diagnosed as a type 1 diabetic and he needed to be treated with insulin. Much later my father died of pancreatic cancer. My family always spoke Greek at home and in the Prahran area where we lived there were many Greek people to talk to. Our family found these early years very difficult, working long hours and late shifts and shifts at different times. Like my father, I believe that hard work gets you results and in the footwear business there are no short cuts.

Yiannakis family and my schooling

In 1962 my parents had their first child: me, Aris. I was followed two years later by a daughter, Helen. I didn't go to a kindergarten, a neighbour or a friend would gather several children at her home four or five days a week. Then I attended Hawksburn Primary School in Malvern Road, which is no longer a school though the building is still there, and then I continued my schooling at the Prahran High School for my secondary education. That school too no longer exists. I did go to Greek school on Saturday afternoons, to help me read and write the language. Today my children are expected to have sufficient Greek to be able to greet their grandparents but not much more than that.

Sporting experiences

At first I played Australian Rules football and soccer. Prahran High School had a very good reputation for its soccer teams, probably due to the Greek population of that area, but not so much for Aussie Rules football. Some students at Prahran High School went on to play for European soccer clubs. I remember playing Aussie Rules football for Prahran High and being beaten by Melbourne High School (where they had budding VFL players in the team) by 30 or 40 goals! Later on I played cricket for six years in the Mercantile League in Albert Park against Port Colts and Cluden. My sister didn't play any sport, Greek girls were expected to stay home and study or help in the house. In general, education was the way to get ahead.

Post-school training and working life

After secondary school I went to Swinburne Technical School and completed 1½ years of a Business Course. I left there when I had the opportunity for a position as a Junior Clerk at the Prahran branch of the National Australia Bank (NAB). Here I progressed from Ledgers to First Teller to Main Teller to Security Clerk. In total I worked for the NAB for six years. I would describe myself as a 'restless youth'. I had got the job at the NAB thanks to my father introducing me to the manager. The job at the bank was good – a clean job, I had to wear a tie and there were social activities including drinks after work. But after returning from a holiday in Europe I knew I wanted to do something for myself in the way my father had, so I decided to go into a trade. When I gave notice to the NAB one of the CEOs offered me a financial incentive to stay in the bank!

My entry into the shoe repairing business

Aris and his father in his first shop at 8 Armstrong Street, c. 1990s

One of my uncles had a very successful business as a shoe repairer in the Hawksburn shopping centre. I had been working for him part-time at the weekends for over a year learning the shoe trade and then after my holiday in Europe I worked with him full-time for a little over a year. In 1987 I saw an ad in the paper for a shoe repair shop for rent in Armstrong Street, Middle Park. I was already familiar to some extent with the shops in Middle Park as the Lemnian Club, to which my family belonged, was located there on the east side of Armstrong Street. When I arrived to inspect the shop it was already occupied by an architect; the owner had advertised for a shoe repairer because he thought the shopping centre needed a shoe repairer because Sam Brown [a well-known local identity and shoe repairer whose shop was in Canterbury Road nearby] was getting older and had a heavy work load. The premises for rent were on the west side of Armstrong Street, opposite the Lemnian Club, and currently occupied by a coffee shop (2016). I had to set up the entire shop with whatever machinery and fittings I needed. I introduced myself to Sam Brown and told him what I intended to do. Sam was happy about this as long as I did a good job. After I opened up and Sam saw that I was doing a good job he encouraged some of his customers to come to me, he also gave me business advice. As my business grew, I asked my landlord if he would like to be involved in an expanded business but he suggested I do this on my own. So I then became a tenant of the Lemnian Society of Victoria at my present location at 3B Armstrong Street.

My marriage and family

In 1989 I was living with my parents in North Caulfield, when I was married to Helen, an Australian girl also of Greek heritage; her family came from the Peloponnese in the south of Greece. Helen's father came from Kalavita, the highest peak there, where it snows. Helen's parents had come to Australia at the same time as my parents, but they had been married in Greece and had a son before they came to Australia. Helen's mother is from Argos in the southern Peloponnese.

Returning to Greece

It took Mother and Father almost 30 years before they returned to Greece.

The Lemnian Society of Victoria

The building in Armstrong Street has been occupied by the Lemnos Society since the 1970s. Prior to the Lemnian Society purchasing the building it had been used as an advertising studio, for photographing cars and the like. I was involved with the Lemnian Youth Society here. Later the building was refurbished making a reception hall downstairs, and upstairs there was a coffee shop/bar where members could go for a drink. To this day the building is still owned by the Lemnian Society, and the downstairs tenants pay rent for their premises including the Tattslotto shop/drycleaners, the gymnasium and my shoe repair business, Aris's Shoe Repairs. The Lemnian Society is now based in Springvale Road, Braeside. It is mainly comprised of senior, retired members with some people of my generation, although I don't go there with my children. The ethos of the Society has changed over the years, although it does support the music and culture of the Lemnian community. The young people are proud of their heritage but have interests outside this culture. Financially the Society is strong but the number of members is declining.

Conducting a business in Middle Park

I have never lived in Middle Park. Running a shoe repair business in Middle Park in my view is that it is not impulse shopping, out of every 100 people who walk past only two or three want to have their shoes repaired. The people who stop at this group of shops only wish to buy a Tattslotto ticket, a newspaper or have their shoes repaired. As Middle Park is an affluent suburb where people are concerned with their appearance the dry cleaners and the shoe repairer do very well. Also people who come into my shop generally buy good quality shoes which are worth repairing and they are not afraid [of the cost] to have them repaired. My customers are predominantly female as they have many more pairs of shoes than men. Repairing these good quality shoes gives me a sense of satisfaction as I can do a better job with leather shoes rather than synthetic ones. I find the Middle Park residents very friendly and loyal to me and my business and I aim to be loyal to them by doing a good job. I have got to know many of the local people in the 20 plus years I have been running this business.

Vicky Galinas

Vasiliki Galinas interviewed at her home in Danks Street by Anne Miller in April 2016. Also present was John Galinas, son of Vasiliki and Thomas. Vasiliki prefers to be called Vicky.

My early life in Greece

I was born in February 1940 in the village of St Dimitrios. The village is close to the town of Katerini which is north of Mount Olympus in northern Greece. I lived with my mother and father and two sisters. I was the middle sister. My father ran a general store in the village and I helped in the store from the time I went to school. My mother didn't work in the store because, though she was very intelligent, she could not read and write. I attended the village school for six years and would come home at lunchtime and

Vicky and her husband Thomas on their wedding day

work in the shop for a couple of hours to give my father a break during the afternoon siesta. I would then go back to school for another couple of hours.

Coming to Australia

My father's friend, who had migrated to Melbourne from Katerini, wrote to him encouraging him to bring the family to Melbourne. Greece was a poor country after the Second World War and many Greek people were going to Melbourne with the idea they could possibly become rich!

The whole family wanted to go to Australia but my mother was very ill with a heart problem. She had open heart surgery and was not strong enough to travel. After six years she passed away. She was very young. I came to Melbourne on my own in March 1962 when I was 22 years old. My younger sister followed in May 1962. We assumed our parents and older sister would come too but this didn't happen. After my mother died, my father and my older sister, her husband and two children all came here.

Vicky with her father, ready to leave Greece for her new life in Melbourne.

My father had paid my fare and I came on the *Patris* with three other girls. It was a very popular ship and we shared two cabins, one up and one down in two bunks. Three of us disembarked in Melbourne but one of the girls went on to Sydney. I was met in Melbourne by my father's friend who had encouraged the family to come here. I did not know him before I came to Melbourne. I stayed with his family for two months until my sister arrived and then we rented a room in South Melbourne. People then would buy a house, keeping one room for themselves and renting out the other rooms. Everyone would share the kitchen and the bathroom.

My father's friends later bought an investment house at 65 Patterson Street where they rented out rooms to people. I and my sister moved in there and we were in charge, still going to work but collecting rents from the other occupants. I lived there for a year and a half.

Finding work in Melbourne

The Australian Government paid new arrivals until they found work. I started doing afternoon shifts from 3pm to 11pm in a factory making dim sims and spring rolls. The factory was called *Wing Lee* and was located in Franklin Street behind the Queen Victoria market. It was owned by Elizabeth Chong's parents. The dim sims and spring rolls were made, not to be sold in the market, but in fish and chip shops. My father's friend used to have a fish and chip shop in Park Street, South Melbourne near the Kingsway Motel, and this is how I got the job at *Wing Lee*. When my sister arrived she worked in a restaurant in Collins Street but I asked my boss at *Wing Lee* if my sister could work with me and he agreed. I stayed there for two years until I was planning to get married.

I marry Thomas Galinas

We met when we both lived at the same house in South Melbourne. Thomas had come to Melbourne in 1956 from the town of Katerini. He was one of five children and his father had died early so Thomas came to Australia to help his family's financial situation back in Greece by sending them some of the money he earned. Thomas had been trained as a patissier in Greece and he made beautiful cakes but, like me, he didn't speak fluent English so he worked at the Tom Piper factory at Port Melbourne. We were married at the Greek Orthodox Church in Victoria Parade in East Melbourne on the corner of Lansdowne Street. We had a wedding party at a restaurant in Elizabeth Street in the reception place upstairs and we invited all our relatives and friends. If we had been married in Greece it would have been more elaborate and the party would have lasted a week, not a day. My wedding dress was loaned to me by the people who took the photographs. We had a day off after the wedding and spent it at the house where we used to live. Then we went back to work on Monday. We stayed in the rented place for another six months and then we bought a house in Hambleton Street on the corner of Mills Street. We moved in one week before Christmas.

Thomas Galinas and family in Greece: (from the left) Thomas's two brothers, Thomas, his widowed mother, his sister (standing), a niece, the eldest brother, an aunt and a cousin.

The Galinas's first home

The new house was a bit primitive: there was no kitchen, internal bathroom or hot water system. We had to heat water by burning wood in the big copper as there was no gas. Gradually Thomas fixed all these things. He is a very competent handyman.

When we first moved to the new house we both took holidays from our regular factory jobs and took temporary jobs at Astor Radio Parts in South Melbourne for those two weeks to make some more money. I was soldering circuit boards but I can't remember what Thomas was doing. We went back to our regular jobs at the end of the two weeks.

Learning English

I learned English from other people, particularly at work, from Dorothy an Australian friend I met on the tram to work and from the television. We had a television at the rented house but it did not have a Greek channel in those days. We had a radio that had a Greek station that broadcast news from home in the evenings and some music.

Children are born

Two years after we were married our first child, John, was born and two years after that Anna our daughter came along. I stopped working when John was born and stayed at home until the children started school.

Returning to work

When both the children started school I got a job at Notts Albert Park Laundry in Mills Street, between Herbert Street and Canterbury Road. I used to take the children to school at Middle Park Primary School and go to the laundry at 9am until 3pm when I would return to the school to collect them. I worked there for 11 years but left when the business was sold to Princes Laundry and closed down. They wanted me to move to their Mentone laundry but it was too far away. I didn't get another job. Modern houses have been built on the original laundry site.

Middle Park Primary School

There were many children of Greek parents at Middle Park Primary. Some families moved out to Oakleigh and Clayton for a larger backyard where they could grow vegetables. Thomas wanted to move too but I didn't drive so we stayed in Middle Park. I travelled everywhere by tram.

Shopping

I shopped mainly at South Melbourne market and the local shops. There used to be a milk bar on the corner of Wright and Hambleton Streets and a butcher in Mills Street and also one in Hambleton Street, Baileys. I seldom went to the Middle Park shops in Armstrong Street.

My father and my older sister

My father and my older sister and her family lived with us for a year in the Hambleton Street house. There were ten people in all and I did the cooking for everybody. Then my older sister and her family bought a house in Albert Park and moved there. My father returned to Greece and then came back in 1992 but he had a big stroke and I nursed him for 15 years. My younger sister lived with us too for seven years, until she married a Greek man in 1969. Then we moved to the house in Danks Street and renovated it. Father moved there with us and I continued to look after him.

Thomas changes jobs

At Danks Street, Thomas continued his cartage work. He had bought a tip truck and become a cartage contractor for Albion Reid when the Tom Piper factory closed. It was very labour intensive work as he had to do his own repairs on the truck to keep it on the road all the time. The council would not let him park the truck outside the Hambleton Street house and so it was parked where the apartments near the Gasworks are now and Thomas would be doing repairs at night.

Going back to Greece

I remember that everyone planned to come to Australia for five years, and in that time they hoped to get rich and return to Greece. But I have been here for 50 years and I do not want to go back to Greece. Thomas and I went back in 1993 for a holiday and I said to Thomas I wish I could close my eyes and wake up in Australia. And Thomas agreed! Although we stayed in Greece for two months, when we landed at Tullamarine I thought it was the happiest day of my life. We did visit St Dimitrios but I had no immediate family there now so people did not recognise me. I have become an Australian citizen and I have only been back to Greece that one time. John and Anna went to Greece by themselves when they finished school.

There are more transcripts on the Middle Park History Group website of oral interviews with other residents of Middle Park who came here from Greece in the 1950s and 1960s: www.middleparkhistory.org

MIDDLE PARK: THE DARK SIDE

Meyer Eidelson

Middle Park may seem a quintessentially sleepy suburb but sometimes appearances can be misleading. It has had its share of notorious events and characters, some of which are described below.

Madame Brussels in Middle Park, 1908

In 1871 Caroline Lohman, later known as 'Madame Brussels' married Studholme George Hodgson in London and emigrated to

Melbourne. Hodgson became a policeman who abandoned Melbourne, and his wife, in 1874. Two years later Caroline Hodgson was operating Melbourne's most refined brothel at 32–34 Lonsdale Street, in the area known as 'Little Lon'. It is immortalised today as Madame Brussels Lane off Lonsdale Street. She owned numerous other brothels as well.

The connection to Middle Park is the mystery of the two houses she owned at 75 and 77 Carter Street. In her will she left them to Martha Burrell, her loyal lieutenant over many years of brothel management.

Martha appears to have lived in one of the properties. What was the purpose of these two properties? Were they discreet brothels in the suburbs? Were they housing for friends and associates? Were they for channelling profits into legitimate property investments? This little mystery has never been resolved.

75 and 77 Carter Street, Middle Park

Madame Brussels herself was the target of vitriol from the self-appointed guardians of the city's morality, particularly male evangelists and *Truth* newspaper. On one occasion she was the subject of a furore that nearly brought down the government when Chief Secretary, Sir Samuel Gillott, was forced to resign because of a financial connection with her and the brothels. The fact that she was a woman successfully running a legal business patronised by wealthy and powerful men only incited more attacks by the 'do-gooders' or 'wowsers' of the day. Wowsers, in case you are interested, is a Melbourne acronym for **We Only Want Our Social Evils Recognised.**

An often-told scandal is the disappearance of the parliamentary mace in 1892. A reward for this unsolved cold case still exists today. Popular rumour was that the mace found its way to Madame Brussels's brothel to be used for un-parliamentary activities. There was also scandal when the government connected a telephone to Madame Brussels's premises. Rumours still exist that tunnels ran from Parliament House under Spring Street to former brothels.

MADAME BRUSSELS IN COURT

REMANDED ON BAIL

MELBOURNE, This Afternoon. Caroline Hodgson, alias Madame Brussells, charged with having been the occupier of a disorderly house in Lonsdale-street, was before the City Court to-day, and was remanded till March 29.

Senior Constable Stapleton yesterday arrested seven other occupants of the house, who were discharged.

Newspaper article from 1906 on Madame Brussels

Madame Brussels was reunited with, and cared for, her first husband George Hodgson in her home 'Gnarwin' at 39 Beaconsfield Parade when he became ill before his death. She joined him in St Kilda Cemetery after she died on 12 July 1908 from a number of health issues.

Bank robbery in Middle Park, 1917

On 18 September 1917, Robert Bennett and Angus Murray robbed the E.S. & A. Bank at 108 Canterbury Road, just south of today's Middle Park Hotel. Armed with a Winchester rifle they tied up the teller, Harold David Brooke, and robbed the bank of 541 pounds saying: '*Throw up your hands or I'll blow your brains out*'.

MIDDLE PARK BANK ROBBERY

ACCUSED COMMITTED FOR TRIAL.

MELBOURNE.—At the South Melbourne Court on Wednesday, Robert Bennett and Angus Murray were charged with having at Middle Park on 18th September, in company, and being armed with a rifle, robbed Harold David Brooke, teller of the E.S. and A. Bank, of £541/11/, the property of the bank. Mr. Sonenberg appeared for the accused.

Detective-Sergeant Coonan stated that when he asked Bennett at Albury how he "got into this scrape," he replied, "I am dead unlucky." He said he had not gone into the bank. On the train Brooke identified Murray as the man who entered the bank, armed. and having gagged him and stole the money. Murray denied this, and said, "I do not think you would know the man. I see by the papers that he wore goggles and spoke with a Yankee accent." Murray added that he left Melbourne on 14th September to visit friends up the country, but refused to say who those friends were. The money, he said, they had won by playing cards on the train.

Newspaper article from 1917 on the bank robbery

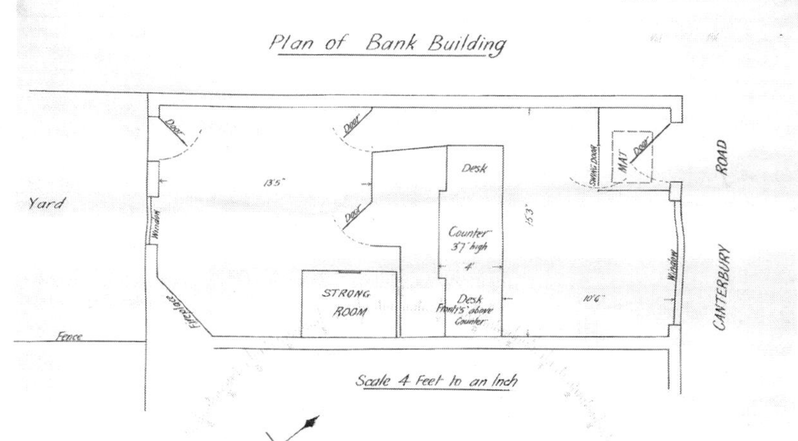

Plans of the E. S. & A. Bank, 1917

Witnesses Mary Edwards, Evelyn Dudfield and Catherine Scott of Middle Park, all identified seeing the men in a 'jinker' or two-wheeled cart in the back lane. Bennett and Murray were sentenced to 15 years gaol.

Angus Murray was an associate of Squizzy Taylor who later organised Murray's escape from Pentridge Gaol in 1923. Taylor had plans for Murray to do a robbery. On 8 October, Murray was charged with the murder of bank manager Thomas Berriman at Glenferrie railway station after 12 policemen in three cars raided Taylor's hideout at 443 Barkly Street, St Kilda. Taylor was also charged with abetting the crime but he escaped conviction. Taylor tried twice more to break Murray out of gaol but failed. Murray was executed for the bank manager's murder despite the crime being masterminded by Taylor.

Squizzy Taylor's first wife was Irene Lorna Kelly of Middle Park. They were married in 1920. At the time of his courtship of Lorna, Taylor's girlfriend was the notorious Dolly Grey, a prostitute from Little Lonsdale Street or 'Little Lon'. Dolly grew suspicious so Taylor hid Lorna in his brother's house at Middle Park but Dolly found her and dragged her off to see Taylor: 'So, who is this then?'

Lorna divorced Taylor in 1924 after he abandoned her for Ira Pender. Lorna was a familiar resident of Middle Park for many years. In 2014, I caught up with Lorna's grandson, Jason Anderson, of Port Melbourne. He told me that only five days before her death, Lorna had told him that his real grandfather was Squizzy Taylor. It was a secret she had hidden well from the family for many years.

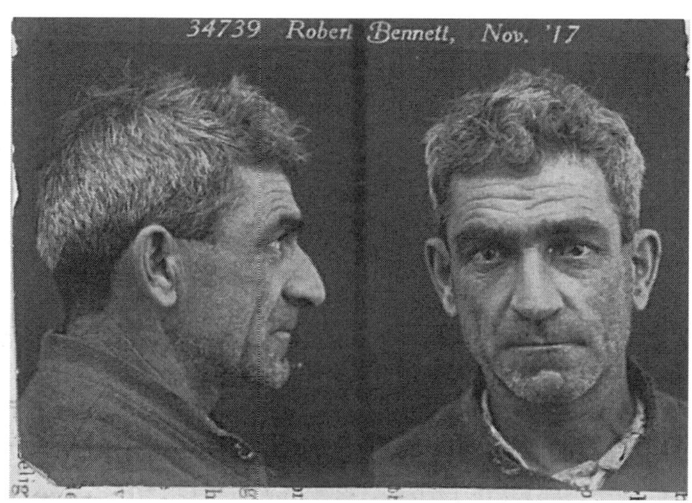

Bank robbers Angus Murray and Robert Bennett

A serial killer in Middle Park, 1942

Chris, a long-time resident of Middle Park, can recall her personal memories of Melbourne experiencing a state of terror due to attacks on women by a serial killer during the Second World War. The streets of Middle Park were made even scarier by the gloom of the 'brownout' with windows at night sealed with brown paper to prevent the houses being targeted by Japanese planes.

Edward Leonski, 1942

The terrifying 'Brownout Strangler', was responsible for the murders of three women during May 1942. Like many Middle Park teenagers, Chris was active in the local Carmelite church social club in Richardson Street. People were vigilant that May and walked together in groups and avoided walking after dark. American soldiers would sometimes chat to them and politely offer to walk them home. Sometimes they accepted but they would always divert them to the wrong address.

Middle Park residents had reason to be fearful because the first of the three murders occurred nearby. Chris believes, in fact, that she and her friends once spotted the murderer in Middle Park. On 3 May 1942, Ivy Violet McLeod, 40, was found badly beaten and strangled on Beaconsfield Parade near Bleak Hotel on the corner of Victoria Avenue. It was evident that robbery was not the motive as she still had her purse.

Leonski's three murder victims

Witnesses eventually picked 24-year-old Edward Leonski, a handsome private in the 52nd Signal Battalion, out of a line-up of American servicemen. His self-confessed motive was that he killed the women to 'get at their voices'.

Leonski had left behind in America a mentally unstable mother, two brothers with prison records and a third in a psychiatric hospital. The American army shipped him to Australia in January 1942 despite the fact that he had tried to strangle a woman while stationed in Texas. Perhaps that is why there was some strenuous opposition when the Curtin government decided to allow the only trial ever to be conducted in Australia under American military law.

Leonski pleaded guilty and was hanged at Pentridge Prison on 9 November 1942. In 1943 artist Albert Tucker, who lived in nearby St Kilda, painted 'Memory of Leonski' in his famous Images of Evil series.

Murder on Middle Park Beach, 1949

One of the most controversial crimes in Melbourne's history occurred near Middle Park beach in 1949 when Elizabeth Maureen

Williams, a 20-year-old typist, was found murdered on the beach south of the Mills Street changing rooms. The case has been the subject of intense debate with repeated calls over the past sixty years for judicial review. It is the subject of an outstanding and recent book *Certain Admissions* by journalist, Gideon Haigh.

Looking west and east along Beaconsfield Parade, Middle Park

Beth Williams lived in Page Street in a share room. On 27 December 1949, she went to Flinders Street Station where  she met John Kerr, a radio announcer and accompanied him to a party. From there they drove to Middle Park arriving about 1.00 am at Danks Street. Kerr never stopped maintaining that he left Beth alive near her house.

Haigh describes Kerr as a poised and charismatic man who was a brilliant witness, a complex character and extremely attractive to women. He was raised in Toorak and educated at Scotch College. Kerr never signed the confession submitted by the police which he always maintained was concocted. The detective who took his statement later went to gaol for corruption. Two juries failed to decide Kerr's guilt but the third jury convicted him. Kerr wrote prolifically and many of his letters were published by the *Argus* in a campaign to re-open his case. He was released after serving 14 years of his sentence and is now deceased.

Barrister Brian Bourke, who now lives in Middle Park, is the longest-practising barrister in Victoria. He had a long legal relationship with Kerr and his family and assisted him and his family personally during and after his release. Brian helped to establish and train the Pentridge debating team of which Kerr was a star performer who represented Victoria in the 1956 Australian debating championships.

Calls have continued in recent years for a posthumous pardon. Today Brian Bourke says Kerr was such a complex character that he still does not have an opinion on his guilt or innocence.

Murder on the run, Beaconsfield Parade, Christmas Eve 1965

In February 2016, Peter Walker aged 74 years was sentenced for crimes of drug, firearms and deception offences. Fifty years previously Walker had spent 19 days on the run with Ronald Ryan – the last man hanged in Australia – after they escaped from Pentridge Prison in Coburg on 19 December 1965. Ryan eventually went to the gallows for the murder of a Pentridge warder, George Hodson, who was shot during the prison break-out.

While on the run Walker shot and killed a tow-truck driver, Arthur Henderson, in a toilet block on Beaconsfield Parade (now demolished). Bizarrely this was near the same location in Middle Park which featured in the murder of Elizabeth Williams in 1949.

Former toilet block corner Beaconsfield Parade and Mills Street

Another Middle Park connection with this crime is Barrister Brian Bourke, mentioned in this book on page 214, who knew Peter Walker and Ronald Ryan well as he had assisted Phillip Opas, QC, at Ryan's murder trial. Bourke and Opas argued that warder Hodson had been accidentally shot by another warder and not by Ryan.

In December 1965, Melbourne was in a state of feverish anxiety about the escapees who were described in the media as highly dangerous. Late on Christmas Eve, Ryan and Walker were at a party at an Elwood flat when Walker left with Henderson to purchase sly-grog in Albert Park. An hour later Walker returned to the party alone, having killed Henderson during an apparent argument. He was convicted of Henderson's manslaughter and imprisoned until 1984.

The hanging of Ryan convulsed Victoria like few other issues and people from all walks of life campaigned to prevent the hanging which nevertheless proceeded at 8.00 am, 3 February 1967. Some today still believe Ryan

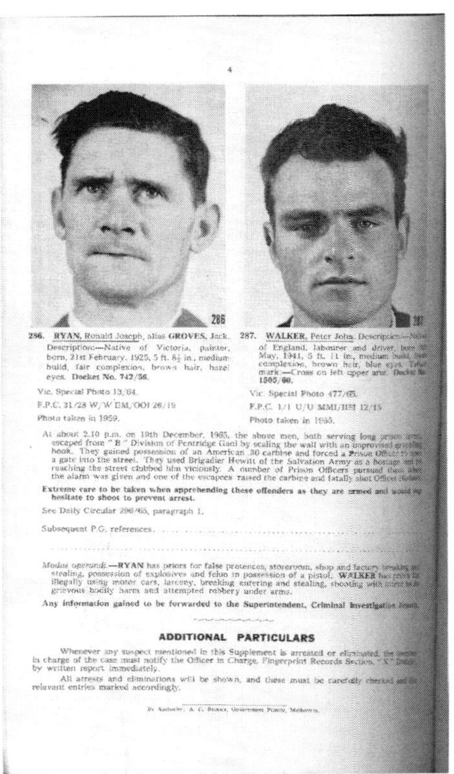

Ronald Ryan and Peter Walker

was innocent. The hanging would probably never have proceeded without the extreme determination of law-and-order Premier, Henry Bolte.

Execution in Middle Park, 2011

One of Victoria's most notorious unsolved crimes occurred in Middle Park on Beaconsfield Parade near Langridge Street at 9.35 pm on 27 February 2011 when racing identity Les Samba, 60, was shot dead by an unknown assailant.

Les Samba's family owned several top racehorses and had success with the 2006 Victoria Derby runner-up, Gorky Park. Samba's daughter Victoria is a former Spring Racing Carnival ambassador.

Les Samba

Mr Samba had travelled to Melbourne for the Premier Yearling Sale on the weekend he died. He left his lodgings at the Crown Metropol for the short drive to Middle Park for a meeting after 9 pm. His killer shot him several times and fled along Langridge Street.

Despite investigation by the Purana taskforce, the murder has not been solved. There has been media speculation that organised crime figures may have been responsible for the planning and execution of the victim. In 2015 police requested that a mystery caller with knowledge of the murder phone them again.

Other calls made to Mr Samba the day before he was murdered, from a Post Office pay phone, are said to hold clues to the killer.

A $1 million reward is in place for information leading to the arrest and successful prosecution of those involved in the killing.

Scene of the murder, Beaconsfield Parade, corner Langridge Street

Explosion in Middle Park, 2014

At 9.16 pm on 4 January 2014 an explosion shattered the peace of a summer evening in Middle Park. Glass and rubble showered onto the pavement as a fireball blew out the windows of a building. The first startled residents to emerge on the street heard the agonised screams of a badly injured policewoman. Within minutes the twilight streets were lit by a fleet of firetrucks, police and SES cars and ambulances.

The drama began after a routine call to police for a welfare check on a resident threatening self-harm in a Hambleton Street unit near the Wright Street corner. Knocks went un-answered, so firefighters climbed to the second-floor balcony. When three police gained entry at 9.16 pm, the unit exploded in flames from an opened gas bottle.

Constable Emma Quick, 29, of St Kilda police station, fought her way out through suffocating smoke and flames to the balcony where she was helped down a ladder by Port Melbourne firefighter Andrew Wood who also suffered burns and trauma. South Melbourne constable Varli Blake, 33, was initially trapped in the room as she fought to get the door open. South Melbourne Sergeant Tony Scully, 53, after checking on the female constables, was treated for severe burns in a shower in one of the units.

Local residents ran to collect hoses and buckets and began dousing the severely burned female constables who lay on the ground floor car park, now transformed into a makeshift emergency room. A resident in pyjamas, coincidentally a doctor at the Alfred Hospital, treated and calmed the victims.

The injured police required intensive treatment at the Alfred Hospital. Emma and Varli were disfigured from the ordeal and faced long and painful rehabilitation after the blast. Sergeant Scully required long-term treatment.

In the following days, flowers piled up on the footpath outside South Melbourne police station. The man accused of triggering the explosion was charged with offences which were later dismissed as the magistrate said the blast was caused by the circumstances of entry.

The three police officers and fireman Andrew Wood were nominated in the Pride of Australia awards for their outstanding bravery. The deputy police commissioner also praised the courageous efforts of Middle Park residents who came to the aid of the wounded.

WAS YOUR HOUSE ONCE A SHOP?

By Sonya Cameron, Diana Phoenix and Rosemary Goad

This list of shops was compiled using Sands & McDougall Melbourne and suburban directories 1857–1974. From 1975 onwards searching continued under categories of shops and businesses using the Melbourne Yellow Pages telephone directory. Once a shop or business no longer appeared in the Yellow Pages under that category it was difficult to ascertain what sort of shop or business took over. If readers can fill in the gaps, or find any errors, please contact the Middle Park History Group.

The street numbers used in this list are the current ones. In about 1903 there was a general re-numbering of the buildings as the suburb expanded.

Armstrong Street

East-South side:

Middle Park Hotel: 1889–2016

Nos 1–3 – built 1907 – rear: Middle Park Theatre from 1918 onwards; front shops: hairdresser, bank, confectioner, kindergarten; above shops: billiard saloon. 1967-1968 Greek Club; 1981 purchased by the Lemnian Brothers Club and though they no longer occupy it, they still own it. No. 1: Middle Park Post Office 1983-1999. Tattslotto Agency 2016; No. 3: confectioner 1976-1983. Aris Shoes 1994-2016

No. 5 (corner Canterbury Place) – grocer (Mrs Emily Love) 1892-1923; grocer 1924-1930; pastry shop 1931-1964; Spotless Laundry/Dry Cleaners 1965-1974. Restaurant 2016

No. 7 – chemist/pharmacy 1909-1974; hairdresser, ladies 1977-1981. Dress shop 2016

No. 9 – ironmonger 1911-1919; dentist 1922-1932; fruiterer 1935-1978. Dry cleaners 2016

No. 11 – dairy produce 1911-1933; pastry goods 1935-1939. Fishmonger 1945-2016

No. 13 – mix of tailor/stationer/confectioner 1911-1926, confectioner 1926-1939; dry cleaners 1940-1942; vacant 1943-1945; South Melbourne public library 1946-1957; shoe shop 1958-1960; ladies' hairdresser 1961-1964; ladies draper 1965; men's wear 1966-1968 ; second-hand dealer 1972-1973; dressmaker/boutique 1974-1976; Middle Park Post Office 2000-2016

No. 15 – dressmaker 1910-1914; costumier 1915-1931; Crofts Stores 1933-1939; frock shop 1940-1946; hairdresser 1950-1954; Master Dry Cleaners 1955-1974. Dress shop 2016

No. 17 (built about 1905) – drapers: 1932-1937 (Sheehan), 1938-1973 (Miller). Chemist 1976-2016

No. 19 (built about 1905) – bootmaker 1926-1939; grocers (Crofts Store) 1940-1970

No. 21 (built about 1905) – butcher 1926-1968

Nos 19–21 – Nancarrow Self Service 1971-1987; Foodmaster 1988; Rite-Way 1989-1998 ; IGA supermarket 2000-2016 (The supermarket was closed during 1999 due to a fire).

No. 23 (corner Richardson St) (built about 1905) – pastry and confectioner 1926-1950. Confectioner/milk bar/take away 1952-2016

No. 53 – confectioner 1900-1912; fruiterer 1920-1935. Flats 1937-2016

West-North side: (numbering changed in 1930)

Nos 2/2A – (up to 1920 listed as part of the chemist on the corner of Canterbury Road which also had a separate listing at 100 Canterbury Road) from 1920-1931 – various shops including pastrycook, fruiterer, florist, confectioner; boot repairer 1932-1960; estate agents 1967-1970; solicitors 1971; stationers manufacturers (Regal Stationers) 1973-1973. Home wares 2016

Nos 4–6 – TAB 1965-2016

No. 8 – fruiterer 1891-1894; bootmaker 1900-1903; dressmaker 1905-1912; milliner 1914-1925; ladies hairdresser 1930-1976. Aris Shoes 1987-1994; Café 2016

Lane

No. 10 – butcher (Watkins) 1892-1956; Middle Park Radio 1958-1983.

No. 12 – bootshop 1898-1942 (main bootmaker was Grenness from 1904-1942); dry cleaners 1943-1969

No. 10–12 – Donlevy's restaurant 1978-1995 (?). (Donlevy Fitzpatrick, who died in 2008, opened his Middle Park restaurant Donlevy's in 1978. It was recognised as Melbourne's first modern cafe-style restaurant). Roti Man Restaurant 2005-2016

No. 14 – fruiterer 1900-1910; confectioner 1911-1942, dressmaker 1945-1962; newsagent with no 16. 1963-1969; stationers (wholesale) 1970-1973; dress shop 1975-1981; ladies hairdresser 1983-1996. Santiago Bar and Restaurant 2016

No. 16 – dairy produce 1891-1895 and 1905-1907; fishmonger 1896-1898. Newsagent 1911-2016

No. 18 – bakery 1891-1960; frocks and knitwear manufacturers 1961-1971; being rebuilt 1974. Internet Marketing Service 2016

No. 20 (corner Erskine Street)– grocer 1905-1924 (James Herschell & Co - also at 36 Mills Street); grocer and wine shop 1925-1930; Wine shop/wine saloon/liquor store retail 1931-2016

No. 22 – newsagent 1905-1909; greengrocer/fruiterer 1910-1990. Wine bar 2016

No. 24 – drapers 1905-1910; painter 1911-1913; ironmonger 1914-1933; florist 1935-1970; take-away food shop 1971-1973; florist 1974-1976. Eng Medical Centre 2016

No. 26 – watchmaker 1905-1913 and confectioner 1908-1963; not available 1965; confectioner 1966-1971; wool shop 1974. Winkle Homewares 2016

No. 28 – estate agents 1907-1928; fishmonger 1929-1937; butcher 1938-1998. Armstrong Street Food Store 2016

No. 30 – butcher 1908-1912; dairy produce 1913-1966 (Flemming family 1925-1954 – granddaughter was Olympic track and field athlete Jane

Flemming); (Estraich family 1957-1971 – post-war European migrants); delicatessen 1967-1978; Armstrong Street Food Store 1994-2016

No. 32 – draper and milliner 1908-1927; hairdresser 1929-1974 (Hugh Cameron 1939-1974). Ladies wear 1979-1990; ladies hairdresser 1988-1990. Loco Food and Drink 2016

No. 34 – dairy produce 1905-1912; butcher 1914-1970 (also Watkins 1926-1961); butcher 1972-1973. Dress shop 2016

No. 36 (corner Richardson St) – drapers (Dowsett 1911-1945), Harris (1946-1953), Dowsett 1954-1960; hardware 1961-1992. Middle Park Video Library 1989-2008; Gum Tree Good Food 2009-2016 and 36a Attico Giftware 2000-2016

No. 38 – pastrycook and confectioner 1911-1932; ironmonger 1937-1954. La Catalana hairdresser 1990-2016

No. 40 – florist 1920-1933; library 1937-1954 (Bookworm's Club);

Nos 38–40 Sykes hardware 1955-1960 (then moved to no. 36); clothing manufacturers 1961-1968; Middle Park Coffee Lounge 1969-1971

No. 42 – cycle shop/costumiere/estate agents 1911-1922; grocer and fruiterer 1923-1968; Goodwill Mission Shop 1972-1973

Nos 40–42 – Goodwill Mission Shop 1974. Le Petit Café 1998-2004; Hot Honey café 2004-2016

No. 82 – confectioner 1926-1974. Dwelling 2016

No. 98a (rear of 98) – ground floor: motor garage 1942-2002; first floor: Scout Hall 1942-1974. Dwelling 2016

Ashworth Street

Nil

Beaconsfield Parade

Nil

Boyd Street

No. 13 – general store/grocer 1889-1961

No. 15 - greengrocer 1892-1895; butcher 1896-1897; wood & coal 1898-1903; fruiterer/greengrocer 1905-1952; dry cleaners 1953. Both shops (13 and 15) have been demolished and replaced by a modern dwelling

No. 20 – bootmaker 1903-1911. Dwelling 2016

No. 23 – dairy 1902-1952. Dwelling 2016

Canterbury Road

South side:

No. 21 – private hospital 1920-1947. Dwelling 2016

No. 36 – laundry 1911-1917. Dwelling 2016

No. 41 – land agent 1900-1907; dressmaker 1908-1915; upholsterer 1917-1923; confectioner 1924-1974. Podiatrist 2016

No. 82 – police station 1915-1924. Dwelling 2016

No. 83 – hat manufacturer (W Elliott Casper) 1908-1930; motor engineer 1932-1964; service station 1965-1968; real estate agents 1970-1971; dealer 1972-1974. Dwelling 2016

No. 84 – Chinese laundry/dry cleaners 1908-1955. Dwelling 2016

No. 85 – confectioner (J. Wilmot) 1910-1937. New dwelling 2016

No. 86 – boot/shoe maker (Sam Brown) 1899-1989. Dwelling 2016

No. 87 – estate agents 1906-1966; AND frocks (retail) 1951-1952; repair service 1953-1963; dealer 1971-1974. Dwelling 2016

No. 88 – manufacturer/factory 1939-1943. Dwelling 2016

No. 96 – estate agents 1904-1981. Dwelling 2016

No. 99 – hairdresser (including Alf Weeks in whose shop the Old Buffers Parade was devised) 1890-1961; snack bar 1963-1969; confectioners 1971-1973

No. 100 – chemist 1899-1974

No 99-100 – bicycle repairs and retail 1977-2009 (The Penny Farthing Cycle Shop); Turner & Lane Homewares 2010-2016; Jack the Geezer Cafe 2016

No. 102 – Middle Park Hotel 1891-2016

No. 104 – State Savings Bank/Commonwealth Bank of Australia 1917-1999. Hair Loss Clinic 2016

No. 106 – motor garage 1911-1996. Psychologist 2016

No. 108 – ES&A Bank 1914–1943; Middle Park Post Office 1914-1965; AND ladies hairdresser 1947-1965; laundrette and dry cleaners 1966-1970

No. 109 – Middle Park Post Office 1966-1970

Nos 108-109 – laundrette and dry cleaners 1971-2016

No. 110 – Moran & Cato, grocers 1914-1959; electrical contractors 1960-1965; Middle Park Post Office 1971-1982. Unknown 2016

No. 111 – fruiterer 1924-1925; draper/soft furnishings (retail) 1939-1962; dry cleaners 1965-1974. Unknown 2016

North side:

Estate agents 1934-1949 ; ES&A Bank/ANZ Bank 1950-1996. Kitchen and bathroom fittings 2016

Middle Park Railway Station

Lakeside Tennis Club 1940-1953

Kerferd Tennis Club 1940-1953

R.S.S. & A.I.L.A. (Returned Sailors', Soldiers' & Airmen's Imperial League of Australia) 1954-1974.

Canterbury Place

North side:

Between Nimmo and Armstrong Streets – vacant 1933; Rugby Hall (St Kilda Rugby Football Club) 1947-1967; motor panel beaters 1955-1957; motor engineers 1960-1965; toy wholesalers 1955-1961; plumbers 1967-1971; knitwear manufacturers 1962-1969

Between Armstrong and McGregor Streets – fuel merchant 1931-1955

Carter Street

North side:

No. 43 – dairy 1902-1908. Dwelling 2016

No. 85 – dairy (Howell) 1891-1907; Motor/cab Proprietor (J Adams) 1908-1928. Dwelling 2016

South side:

No. 86 – dairy 1900-1961 (Grierson 1900-1911; Farnsworth's Parkside Dairy 1912-1951, Woodruffs Royal Dairy 1952-1961). NOTE – stables' address is 107 Hambleton Street. Dwelling 2016

Danks Street/Patterson Street

South side:

No. 372 Danks – Police Station 1912-1917. Dwelling 2016

No. 36 Patterson Street – Asbestos factory 1902-1989 (Manager: Mr Henry J Pask, Tucks Asbestos Company) (1968-1974 also at 38a Langridge Street). Dwellings 2016

North side:

No. 337 Danks – dairy (Mullligan) 1918-1938; Mrs Mulligan 1939-1974. Dwelling 2016

Nos 381-383 Danks – Federal Building Material Co Tile co (Manager: John Crotty) 1905-1912. No listing 1913-1936; Listowel flats 1937-2016.

No. 45 Patterson Street – dairy (W H Feign) 1908-1940; Mrs Feign 1941-1957. Dairy has sometimes been listed as at 45 Langridge Street and the dwelling there now has that address.

No. 69 Patterson Street – police station 1932-1969. This was the last police station in Middle Park. These smaller police stations were a drain on police resources and not always open. They were replaced by the larger police stations such as that in Banks Street, South Melbourne. Dwelling 2016

Erskine Street

North/East side:

No. 71 (cnr Wright Street) Beale's Steam Laundry 1911-1965. There are no houses at nos. 71-75 Erskine Street. Instead there is a block of flats at 92 Hambleton Street which goes through to Erskine Street. The laundry was listed as at 92 Hambleton Street from 1905-1917.

No. 75 – Jensen & Larsen paint manufacturer 1920-1927; wood/storage yard 1928-1936

South/West side:

None

Fraser Street (boundary of Middle Park)

West side:

Nil

Hambleton Street

North side:

No. 99 – dairy (Mrs Annie Howell) 1908-1920; 1921-1941 entries just state Annie Howell's name. This may not have been a dairy but a dairy produce shop. Dwelling 2016

No. 107 on the corner of Harold Street are the stables of the dairy at no. 86 Carter Street.

Nos 109-111 – grocer/general store/licensed grocer/liquor store retail 1884-1991 (Cunningham's grocer, wines and spirits 1889-1965). Dwelling 2016

No. 113 – butcher 1900-1983 (W. Cazaly 1907-1916, Anderson & Bailey 1917-1935 then just Baileys 1936-1983). Dwelling 2016

No. 115 – draper 1889-1917; grocer 1924-1974; milk bar 1976; butcher 1985-1988. Dwelling 2016

No. 117 – confectioner 1891-1897; Chinese laundry 1903-1932. Dwelling 2016

No. 119 – bootmaker 1894-1937. Dwelling 2016

No. 121 – various – grocer/greengrocer/dairy/confectioner 1896-1936. Dwelling 2016

No. 123 – dairy/grocer/fruiterer/greengrocer 1892-1945. Dwelling 2016

South side:

No. 6 – laundry (A Wallace) 1909-1955. Dwelling 2016

No. 92 – Beale – IXL Middle Park Laundry 1905-1917 – see its listing at its 71 Erskine Street address

Harold Street

East side:

No. 5 – woodyard/fuel merchant 1886-1971; nos. 5-7 flats 1972-2016.

West side:

No. 62 – Mardell's hat factory 1899-1935; Alandale Flats 1937-2016

Herbert Place

Nil

Herbert Street

South side:

No. 10 – dairy (Martin Dobeli) 1908-1935; Hambleton Dairy 1936-1937. Dwelling 2016

Nos 24-26 – woodyard (J Page/W Laycock) 1908-1937; Hambleton Dairy 1938-1947; Morris Brothers Union Dairy 1948-1957; stables 1958-1960; carpet service/carpet layers 1961-1985. Dwelling 2016

No. 46 – woodyard and fruiterer/grocer/pastry shop 1889-1928; library 1935-1937; frock shop 1949-1959.

No. 48 – bootmaker 1892-1923; vacant 1924-1928; grocer 1935-1936; bicycle retail 1951-1959.

Nos 46-48 woodyard 1929-1934; bicycle retail 1960-1971. Converted to one dwelling 1980s. Dwelling 2016

No. 54 – butcher/smallgoods/fishmonger 1886-1923; boot repairer 1924-1945.

No. 56 – dairy 1894-1904, confectioner 1905-1974.

Nos 54-56 – Dwelling 2016

North side:

No. 15 – newsagent 1895-1910; confectioner 1912-1918; bootmaker 1919-1922. Dwelling 2016

No. 39 – Phelam Saunders (Ladies Kindergarten School) 1903-1910. Dwelling 2016

Kerferd Road

No. 63 (cnr Herbert Street) – Melbourne Tram and Bus Co, 1889-1890; wood and coal yard 1897-1907. Dwelling 2016

No. 65 – South Melbourne Cooperative Laundry, 1893-1906. Dwelling 2016

No. 75 – grocer 1889-1893; Dobeli (dairy) 1905-1907. Dwelling 2016

No. 109 – newsagent/stationer 1897-1963; dry cleaners 1969-1974. Dwelling 2016

No. 111 – various occupiers – greengrocer/grocer but mostly a confectioner 1900-1969; milk bar 1971-1993. Dwelling 2016

Langridge Street

East side:

No. 45 – former dairy – see listing under No. 45 Patterson Street

West side:

No. 38 – livery stables 1908-1919, boatbuilder/fishing tackle/nets (Savage/Oxley) 1920-1967. Dwelling 2016

No. 38a – Tucks Asbestos Factory 1968-1974 (factory at 36 Patterson Street)

No. 42a – dairy produce 1914-1927, general store/grocer 1930-1943, confectioner 1945-1947; grocer 1948-1965; confectioner 1966-1969; milk bar 1972-1979. Dwelling 2016

Little Page Street

North side:

Between Kerferd Road and Boyd Street; woodyard/fuel merchant 1931-1954

South side:

No. 74 (between Mills and Wright Streets) – cabinet maker (Reeves) 1928-1965. Private dwelling 2016

Nos 202-208 (formerly no. 48) (between Armstrong and McGregor Streets (factory, built 1926) – button manufacturers 1927-1930; milk bottle top manufacturers (Australian Seal Co) 1929-1954; vacant 1955-1957; storage and transport facility (various companies) and office for an architectural company 1958-1974; converted to a private dwelling in the 1990s. Dwellings 2016

McGregor Street

West-North side:

Nos 14-18 – woodyard 1911-1936. Dwelling 2016

East side:

No. 13 – grocer 1904-1991. Dwelling 2016

Mills Street

East-South side:

No. 25 – Butcher, 1935-1974 (A McGregor 1938-1955). Buyer agents 2015

No. 27 – grocer, 1936-1960; confectioner 1961-1962; oil burners 1968-1969; second hand furniture 1970-1973. Albert Park Pet Supply 1988. Children's shoe shop 2016

No. 29 – cake shop and confectioner, 1936-1946 – Dunn & McKendrick 1936-1938, pastries/cakes (Bisset and Browne 1939-1945), pastries/cakes 1946-1953; vacant 1954-55; cakes 1956-1960; not available 1961; fruiterer 1962-1973

Nos 27-29 second hand dealer 1974-1978. Ladies dress shop 2016

No. 31 – hairdresser 1936-1994. Ladies dress shop 2016

No. 39 – fruiterer 1927-1930; butcher 1932-1933; fruiterer 1935; butcher 1936-1942. Dwelling 2016

No. 41 – confectioner, 1905-1921. Dwelling 2016

No. 147 (consists of shop and dwelling) confectioner, 1930-1946; tailor 1968-2015. Dwelling 2016

No. 147a – library 1940-1960

No. 153a – fishmonger 1939-1968

No. 153 – confectioner/milk bar 1935-1979. Unknown 2016

No. 155 – dairy produce, 1938-1962; delicatessen 1963-1974; florist, 1976-1983. Unknown 2016

No. 157 – chemist, 1928-1974. Small business 2016

No. 159 – fruiterer, 1930-1976 (may also have been a confectioners for short time). Chiropractor 2016

No. 161 (2 shops) – butcher, 1927-1977 and grocer, 1927-1974; second hand dealer 1979-1991; hair salon and Aurora Travel 2016

No. 163 – house 1907-1956, apartments 1957-1974; milk bar 1980-2016

No. 165 – dwelling and shop, Bissett and Browne, confectioners, 1938-1946 and lock-up shop, hairdresser, 1937-1949; confectioner and hairdresser, 1950-1960; confectioner/milk bar 1961-1971; Jimmy's Pizza Bar 1972-1994; Ragazzi's Italian Restaurant 1995-2016

West-North side:

Nos 4-14 – Grey's Steam Laundry/Nott's Albert Park Steam Laundry, 1901-1987. Replaced by townhouses.

No. 32 – greengrocer/fruiterer 1890-1968 (Thompson's 1900-1943). Dwelling 2016

No. 34 – mostly a butcher, particularly from 1905-1946 (James Baster 1905-1928, J. Grennan 1930-1946); Dry Cleaners 1947-1964; Peter's Hardware 1965-1968. Dwelling 2016

No. 36 – grocers, 1883-1925 (James Herschell & Co 1891-1925 – James Herschell & Company operated many grocery stores in South Melbourne including one at 20 Armstrong Street. Their main store was on the corner of Park and Ferrars); wine café/saloon/wine retail/wine cellars 1926-2007. Restaurant 2016

No. 42 – fruiterer, 1897-1903; bootmaker, 1904-1925; confectioner, 1926-1960

No. 44 – various – blacksmith, confectioner, general store, dairy produce, grocer 1895-1974; milk bar 1976-1977

Nos 42-44 – McGain's Albert Park Nursery 1979-1983; Peter Poynton's Albert Park Nursery 1984-2004

Nos 36-44 were demolished in about 2008 and replaced with a mixture of shops with apartments above

No. 46 – fruiterer, 1904-1913; hairdresser, 1929-1971

No. 48 – various until 1915; grocer, 1916-1942; butcher 1943-1976.

Nos 46-48 – Port Phillip Animal Hospital 2007-2016

Nos 50-52 – dressmaker then bootmaker, 1890-1898; nothing listed 1899-1925; boot repairer 1926-1935; Physiotherapist 2002-2016

No. 50 only: boot repairer 1936-1964; not available 1965-1966; builders 1967-1971

No. 52 only: dressmaker 1936-1953; chiropodist 1954-1956; (no. 52a library 1940-1945; watch maker 1946-1957); Leisure Library 1957-1960; plumber 1962-1965; watch makers 1967–1971. Coin Laundrette 1972-1974

No. 74 – grocer, 1928-1951 ; fruiterers 1952; not listed as a shop 1953-1959; not available 1960; Real Estate Agency 1961-1978 (Dennis Realty). Dwelling 2016

No. 92 – newsagent, 1910-1983 (cnr Richardson Street) (Laycocks 1913-1919) and Middle Park West Post Office – 1943-1981. Dwelling 2016

No. 94 – pastry shop/bakery, 1926-1977. Dwelling 2016

No. 132 – butcher, 1929-1962; not available 1963-1964; beauty salon/ladies hairdresser 1965-1985. Dwelling 2016

No. 136 – dairy produce 1956-1973. Bicycle repairs and retail 1977-1988. Unknown 2016

No. 138 – fruiterer, 1941-1974. Unknown 2016

No. 170 – grocer 1894-1963; confectioner, 1964; not available 1965-1966; confectioner 1967; commercial artist 1971-1974. Dwelling 2016

Neville Street

North side:

No. 17 – oil merchant 1914-1923; manufacturers of butchers' supplies (Lixie Pty Ltd) 1924-1969; air conditioning manufacturers 1970-1976. Dwelling 2016

Nos 131-137 – Honeybone's Hall 1906-1922. Dwelling 2016

No. 131 only – Corio Prep School 1919-1922; Methodist school/kindergarten 1923-1967

Nos 145-151 – Honeybone's Hat Manufacturers 1892-1940. Dwelling 2016

No. 145 – vacant 1941-1942; electrical engineers 1943-1945 ; Air Department 1946-1949; P.M.O. workshop 1950-1960; knitwear manufacturers 1961-1963

South side:

Nos 136-142 – hat block manufacturers (Godfrey Hat Block Co.) 1913-1977. Dwelling 2016

Nimmo Street

East-South side:

No. 7 – estate agents 1889-1897. Dwelling 2016

No. 21 – dairy (also sometimes: confectioner & dairy and store & dairy) 1896-1930; grocer 1931-1969. Dwelling 2016

No. 23 – grocer 1895-1922; boot repairs 1925-1940; furriers 1954-1955; opportunity shop 1956-1961. Dwelling 2016

No. 37 – grocer – 1906-1949 (M.E. O'Dwyer) ; grocer 1950-1973; confectioner/milk bar 1974-1978. Dwelling 2016

No. 53 – Wood, coal and coke yard 1913-1935; became Florence Court flats in 1937. Dwelling 2016

West-North side:

No. 44 – bakery 1907-1941. Subsequently listed under 254-156 Richardson Street. Originally Coppard Bros Bakery, then Gillespie's Bakery from 1925-1941.

Page Street

North/East side:

Nil

South/West side

Nos 104/106 (cnr Boyd Street) – grocer (Oldfield) 1893-1955. Dwelling 2016
No. 166 (cnr Harold Street) – Mardell straw hat factory 1907-1934; laundry 1935-1946. Dwelling 2016

Park Grove

Nil

Park Road

North side:

None

South side:

No. 88 – butcher 1928-1983. Dwelling 2016
No. 90 (cnr Fraser Street) – grocer 1911-1974. Dwelling 2016

No. 90a – confectioner and cakes 1923-1929; fruiterer 1930-1974. Dwelling 2016

Richardson Street

North side:

No. 163 – grocer 1947-1960; confectioner 1961-1974. Dwelling 2016

No. 193 – greengrocer 1907-1914; confectioner 1916-1969. Dwelling 2016

No. 247 – greengrocer 1891-1898, bootmaker 1903-1912, greengrocer 1913-1917, clothes cleaner 1920-1923; boot repairer 1925-1936; ladies hairdresser 1937-1960. Small business 2016

No. 251 – newsagent 1905-1909, butcher 1913-1935; vacant 1936; fishmonger 1937-1942; pastry shop 1948-1968. Restaurant 2016

No. 253 – hairdresser 1909-1928 ; grocer 1929-1935; dairy produce 1936-1961; beauty salon 1964-1965; boot repairer 1969-1974. Dwelling 2016

No. 253 a-c – shops below some flats – various occupants over the years: dietitian, upholsterer, chiropodist, radio dealer, milliner, fruiterer, dressmaker, frock shop, beauty salon/ladies hairdresser/real estate agents 1937-2016

No. 259 – Middle Park Police Station 1925-1931. Dwelling 2016

No. 273 – draper 1918-1938; fruiterer 1949-1957. Dwelling 2016

No. 275 – fruiterer/greengrocer 1892-1912; grocer 1913-1915; fishmonger 1916-1926; caterer 1927-1934; confectioner 1935-1971. Dwelling 2016

South side:

No. 248 – police station 1896-1915. Dwelling 2016

Nos 254-256 – Coppard's Bakery 1910-1925 – for more details see entry under 44 Nimmo Street. Later reverted to this address as the Middle Park Community Centre 1957-2016

No. 274 – fruiterer/wood and coal yard 1904-1909; grocer 1914-1931; pastry shop 1932; boot repairer 1933-1942; grocer 1947-1978; radio repairs and service 1985-1988. Beauty salon 2016

No. 276 – fishmonger/poultry 1918-1926; fishmonger 1927-1936; Library 1937-1943. Unknown 2016

No. 278 – fruiterer 1910-1976. Unknown 2016

No. 280 – dairy produce 1910-1967. Unknown 2016

No. 302 – boot maker 1906-1918. Dwelling 2016

No. 310 – general store/grocer 1891-1935; fruiterer 1936-1943. Small business 2016

No. 364 – grocer/wine & spirits 1891-2016

No. 366 – bootmaker/boot repairer 1915-1961; dry cleaning 1962-1967; fruiterer 1968-1973; confectioner 1974. Dwelling 2016

Wright Street

East side:

No. 9 – confectioner 1903-1961. Dwelling 2016

No. 15 – bootmaker/boot repairer 1889-1954. Dwelling 2016

No. 71 – confectioner 1894-1960. Dwelling 2016

No. 111 – grocer 1923-1983. Dwelling 2016

West side:

No. 8 – grocer 1887-1967. Dwelling 2016

No. 34 – grocer 1891-1938; confectioner 1939-1949; grocer 1950-1951; confectioner 1952-1974. The Melbourne Yellow Pages do not record what type of shop was operating after 1974. After a period of closure, local residents state that it was operating as a milk bar at the end of the 1980s until 1996 when it finally closed. The house was demolished and two town houses were built. The current address is 87 Hambleton Street.

No. 56 – grocer 1910-1946. Dwelling 2016

Young Street

Nil

MAP OF MIDDLE PARK SHOPS
AND LIGHT INDUSTRIES

Middle Park shops
and light industries
KERFERD ROAD
YOUNG STREET
HERBERT PLACE
CANTERBURY PLACE
HERBERT STREET
CANTERBURY PLACE
CARTER STREET
CANTERBURY PLACE
HAMBLETON STREET
ERSKINE STREET
RICHARDSON STREET
MILLS STREET
HAROLD STREET
ROW
BOYD STREET
NEVILLE STREET
NEVILLE ST
PAGE STREET
LITTLE PAGE STREET
DANKS STREET
WRIGHT STREET
LITTLE FINLAY STREET
MERTON PLACE
JOHNSON LANE

AUGHTIE DRIVE
CANTERBURY PLACE
CANTERBURY ROAD
NIAMO STREET
ARMSTRONG STREET
MCGREGOR STREET
PARK ROAD
LANGRIDGE STREET
FRASER STREET
PATTERSON STREET
ASHWORTH STREET
STREET
Shaded areas show location of shops and light industries

REFERENCES AND FURTHER READING

Shops and shopping in Middle Park: changes over 100 years

Cairns, Tom. *Grocer boy : Middle Park 1933–1939.* City of Port Phillip Library, 1989.

Davison, Graeme. *Car Wars : How the Car Won Our Hearts and Conquered Our Cities.* Allen & Unwin, Crows Nest, NSW 2004.

Kingston, Beverley. *Basket, Bag and Trolley : a history of shopping in Australia.* Oxford University Press, Melbourne, 1994.

Linnett, Ken. Fifty years of service … but off the hook at last. IN *Emerald Hill & Sandridge Times,* 6 October 1983, p. 5.

Middle Park History Group. Personal histories. http://www.middleparkhistory. org/personal-histories. Accessed 18 September 2016.

Sands & McDougall's Directory of Victoria [Uniform title] 1857–1974. Sands & McDougall, Melbourne, 1857–1974.

Smith, Charlotte H. (2005) *Domestic Refrigeration & Refrigerators in Museum Victoria Collections.* http://collections.museumvictoria.com.au/articles/710. Accessed 18 September 2016.

Smoke Abatement Devices, *Age,* 4 May 1912, p. 17.

Toni Risson's Blog. https://tonirisson.wordpress.com/. Accessed 18 September 2016.

Writer, Larry (29 January 2013). *Nostalgia alert : our favourite lollies.* Sydney Morning Herald. http://www.smh.com.au/lifestyle/home/food/nostalgia-alert-our-favourite-lollies-20130129-2djtv.html. Accessed 18 September 2016.

Yellow Pages Melbourne [Uniform title], 1975–2010. Telecom Australia, Melbourne, 1975–2010.

Young, John and Spearritt, Peter. (2008, July) *Supermarkets and Grocers.* http://www.emelbourne.net.au/biogs/EM01450b.htm. Accessed 18 September 2016.

Dairies, manufacturing and other light industries

'Albert Park Steam Laundry.' IN *Jubilee history of the City of South Melbourne and illustrated handbook*. Periodicals Publishing Co. [Melbourne] 1905. p. 170.

'Mayor's visit to laundry : Beale & Co's, Middle Pk.' IN *Record*, 31 July, 1926, p. 6.

'Federal Building Material Company.' IN *Cyclopedia of Victoria : an historical and commercial review, descriptive and biographical facts, figures and illustrations, an epitome of progress*. Edited by James Smith, Cyclopedia Company, Melbourne 1903. pp. 156–157.

Social changes and development in Middle Park

Cannon, M, *The Land Boomers*, Melbourne University Press, Melbourne, 1967.

Morris, G, *No 2815. Middle Park School, 1887–1987*, Middle Park Primary School, 1987.

Priestley, Susan, *South Melbourne: A History*, Melbourne University Press, Melbourne, 1995.

Middle Park: a beachside suburb

Barnard, J. *Jetties and piers – A background history of maritime infrastructure in Victoria*, Heritage Victoria, 2008.

Dayley, C, *The History of South Melbourne: from the foundation of settlement at Port Phillip to the year 1938* by order for the Council of the City of South Melbourne, 1940.

Priestley, S. *South Melbourne: A History*, Melbourne University Press, Melbourne, 1995.

Grogan, R, *Commodores, Colonials and Councillors*, Cygnet, Melbourne, 2007.

Morris, G, *No. 2815. Middle Park School, 1887-1987*, Middle Park Primary School, 1987.

The Middle Park Bowling Club

The author, David South, researched most of the information for this chapter from Club Annual Reports, which for most years are stored in bound volumes at the Club. Handwritten Committee minutes are available from 1915. Copies of *The Bowler* magazine (which was a weekly published by McNeill and Bruce of Melbourne from 17 October 1908 to 24 April 1913) are held in the RVBA Archives from 1910, as is a complete set of *Bowls* magazine (published weekly from 23 October 1924 by Bowlers Publications, Melbourne, from 16 October 1931 by Wilke and Co, Melbourne, and more recently as a monthly by the RVBA). The assistance of Bill Sorraghan OAM, RVBA historian and archivist, in accessing these is acknowledged. A number of Middle Park Club members also helped a good deal, particularly Peter Anderson.

Middle Park and the Great War

Primary sources

Discovering Anzacs [Online service records from the National Archives]
Cecil McAnulty's *Diary*, Australian War Memorial (online).
Jim Makin's *Wartime Diary and Letters*, Perce Makin's private collection.
Les Makin's *Wartime Letters*, Australian War Memorial (online) and Perce
  Makin's collection.
World War I, Middle Park History Group (MPHG) website.
The *Record*, South Melbourne's local paper (online).

Secondary sources

Beaumont, Joan, *Broken Nation – Australia in the Great War*, Allen & Unwin,
  2014.
Bennett, Scott, *Pozieres – The Anzac Story*, Scribe, Melbourne, 2011.
Burness, Peter, *The Nek – A Gallipoli Tragedy*, Exisle Publishing, Wollombi,
  NSW, 2012.
Engelos, Lambis, 'My Quest to Find the 'Missing', in *Wartime* 2008 (online).
Englezos, Lambis, 'The Missing Soldiers of Fromelles', Online recording of an
  address to the Nepean Historical Society 2016.
Fitzpatrick, Kathleen, *Solid Bluestone Foundations*, Macmillan Australia,
  Melbourne, 1983.
Grey, Jeffrey *A Military History of Australia*, Cambridge University Press,
  Melbourne, 1990.
Grossman, Dave, *On Killing – The Psychological Cost of Learning to Kill in War
  and Society*, Back Bay Books, New York, 2009.
Lindsay, Patrick, *Fromelles*, Hardie Grant Books, Melbourne, 2008.

Middle Park – From Swamp to Suburb, Middle Park History Group 2014.

Travers, Richard, *Diggers in France,* ABC Books, Sydney, 2008.

Wilson, Maree, *Never Forget Uncle Les,* Self published (Booklet available from the Middle Park History Group and the Emerald Hill Heritage Centre.)

The Greek immigrants of Middle Park

Australian Bureau of Statistics. Census, *Community Profiles*, 1996, 2001, 2006, 2011. (http://www.abs.gov.au/websitedbs/censushome.nsf/home/communit yprofiles?opendocument&navpos=230)

City of Port Phillip. *Overseas born – year of arrivals.* (http://profile.id.com.au/ port-phillip/overseas-born-by-year-of-arrivals). Accessed 19 October 2016.

De Stoop, Dominique François. *The Greeks of Melbourne.* Transnational, Melbourne, 1996.

Tamis, Anastasios Myrodis. *The Greeks in Australia.* Cambridge University Press, Port Melbourne, 2005.

Middle Park: the dark side

Haigh, Gideon, *Certain Admissions: A Beach, A Body, and a Lifetime of Secrets,* Penguin ebook, 2015.

Richards, M. *The Hanged Man: the life and death of Ronald Ryan,* Scribe, 2002.

Saunders, Kay. *Notorious Australian Women,* Harper Collins, Sydney, 2011.

ILLUSTRATIONS

The authors and publisher have made every endeavour to trace and acknowledge the copyright holders of the photographs, diagrams, maps and illustrations reproduced in this book. If we have failed to acknowledge any printed material please contact us at middleparkhistory.org and we will seek to redress the situation.

Social changes and development in Middle Park — Page No.

Middle Park: a beachside auburb — Page No.

History of the Middle Park Bowling Club   **Page No.**

Middle Park and the Great War   **Page No.**

The Greek immigrants of Middle Park   Page No.

All images reproduced with permission of the interviewees

Middle Park: the dark side   Page No.

Front and back cover

Front cover:

Middle Park Baths, c 1920. Images of Yesteryear (https://www.
   imagesofyesteryear.com.au/products/view/middle_park_05m)

Back cover:

Laycock's Newsagency, c. 1915, 92 Mills Street, Albert Park, 3206,
   courtesy Tim Jomartz Collection (posted to Facebook 21 December
   2013)

Vicky farewelling her father at Piraeus, Greece, 1962. Courtesy Vicky
   Galinas

Beaconsfield Parade, Middle Park, c. 1920. Images of Yesteryear (https://
   www.imagesofyesteryear.com.au/products/view/middle_park_02p)